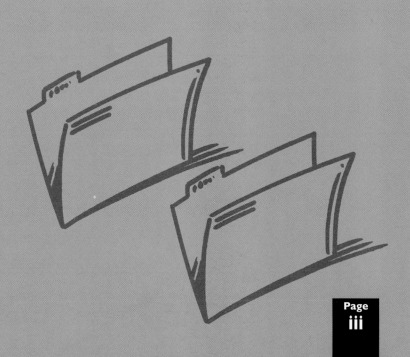

easy

Microsoft®
Excel 97,
Second Edition

See it done

Do it yourself

que®

Trademarks

Executive Editor
Jim Minatel

Acquisitions Editor
Stephanie McComb

Development Editor
Lorna Gentry
Nancy D. Warner

Technical Editor
Kyle Bryant

Managing Editor
Thomas F. Hayes

Project Editor
Shanon Martin

Copy Editor
Malinda McCain

Indexer
Chris Barrick

Production Designer
Lisa England

Proofreader
Betsy Deeter

Book Designer
Jean Bisesi

Cover Designer
Anne Jones

Illustrator
Bruce Dean

How to Use This Book

It's as Easy as 1-2-3

Each part of this book is made up of a series of short, instructional lessons, designed to help you understand basic information that you need to get the most out of your computer hardware and software.

Click: Click the left mouse button once.

Double-click: Click the left mouse button twice in rapid succession.

Right-click: Click the right mouse button once.

Pointer Arrow: Highlights an item on the screen you need to point to or focus on in the step or task.

Selection: Highlights the area onscreen discussed in the step or task.

Click & Type: Click once where indicated and begin typing to enter your text or data.

Tips and Warnings give you a heads-up for any extra information you may need while working through the task.

2 Each task includes a series of quick, easy steps designed to guide you through the procedure.

How to Drag: Point to the starting place or object. Hold down the mouse button (right or left per instructions), move the mouse to the new location, then release the button.

Drag

Drop

1 Each step is fully illustrated to show you how it looks onscreen.

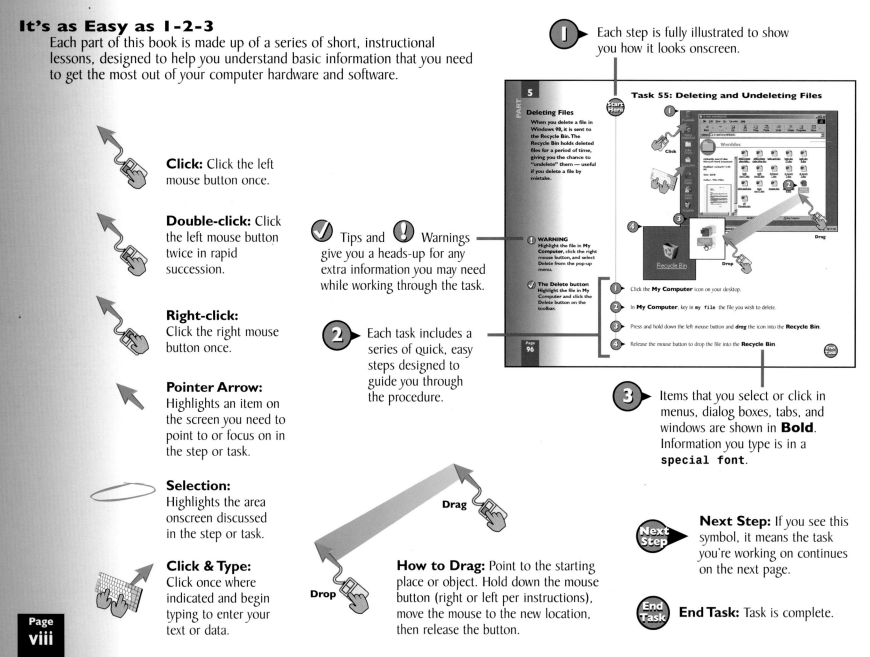

3 Items that you select or click in menus, dialog boxes, tabs, and windows are shown in **Bold**. Information you type is in a `special font`.

Next Step: If you see this symbol, it means the task you're working on continues on the next page.

End Task: Task is complete.

Introduction to Excel 97

A software surprise used to be like a practical joke, which is to say not very funny and not at all practical. Sometimes a program wouldn't do what we wanted it to do. Sometimes a program ground to a halt and didn't do anything at all. But now that computers—bristling with crisp color, stereo sound, and CD-ROMs—have gotten more sophisticated, software has grown up as well.

Excel is a case in point. Excel 97 is still good for a surprise or two, but the surprises are entirely pleasant.

You expect a spreadsheet program such as Excel to be a super-calculator, but Excel is also a word processor for numbers, capable of manipulating and formatting your data in myriad ways.

Excel is a powerful database program, although Excel calls them lists. You can filter lists to display only the data you want to see, and you can summarize long lists of data, with subtotals, grand totals, and pivot tables. Excel is also a graphics tool, data organizer, and numbers analyzer. It can calculate a mortgage payment, manage a phone list, and help forecast next year's earnings.

All of which may be impressive, though not surprising—after all, we expect a lot from our software. But Excel also includes a few things you might not have anticipated. You'll find animated paint brushes, contortionist paper clips, 3D lighting effects, and cameo appearances by a Shakespeare stand-in and an Einstein-like genius. Excel also provides a direct connection to the world of information and entertainment on the Internet. While these Excel gadgets are not strictly necessary for calculating tables of numbers, they are extremely useful—and fun.

Few of us, of course, are paid to have fun. We still need Excel to help us crunch numbers, analyze data, and produce charts. We rely on Excel to manage databases and to pep up our work with dazzling graphics. We also want to do all these things in time to be home for dinner. That's where Easy Excel 97 comes in. It's written and designed to show you exactly how to do what you need to do, clearly and simply, no matter how complex the task. Easy Excel 97 will help you get through your work with ease, for results that will surprise you—pleasantly.

PART I

Introducing Excel

Excel is a powerful and capable spreadsheet program that's also easy to use. A passing acquaintance with the program's basic terms and features is both quickly gained and amply rewarded. Excel can do a surprising number of things, and its speed and ease are unleashed by a very small amount of practice.

Part I of this book is the place to gain an introduction to Excel and to practice some of the basic techniques essential to running the program. When you've absorbed the fundamentals in Part I, you'll be on your way toward making Excel a tool as useful as it is capable.

Tasks

Task 1: Starting Excel

Open the Excel Program

With Excel installed on your computer, a mighty calculating machine is three mouse-clicks away, no matter what else you happen to be working on. And if that's one more click than you'd like, a simple trick puts Excel within two clicks instead.

✓ **Use the Shortcut Icon**
If an Excel shortcut icon is on your Windows desktop, you can use it to start Excel. Click the icon once if you are using Windows 98 or using Windows 95 with Internet Explorer 4; double-click if you are using Windows 95 without Internet Explorer 4.

✓ **Starting Excel from Windows 98 or from Windows 95 with IE4**
If you are using Windows 98 or using Windows 95 with Internet Explorer 4, you can create a shortcut on the Quick Launch toolbar to access Excel faster.

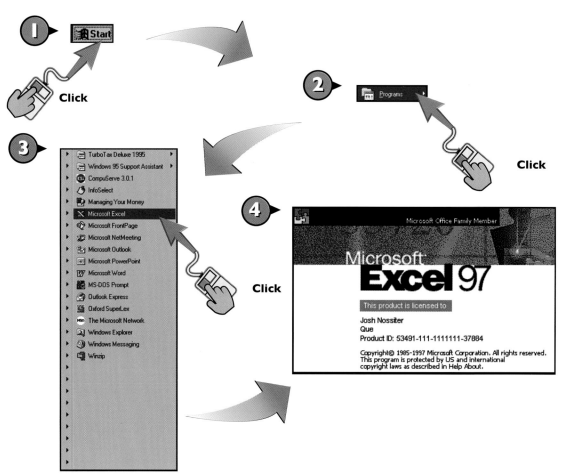

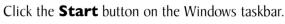
Click the **Start** button on the Windows taskbar.

Choose **Programs** on the Start menu.

Choose **Microsoft Excel** from the list of programs.

Wait a moment or two while the program loads; when the Excel 97 splash screen disappears, you're ready to use Excel.

Task 2: Using the Excel Screen

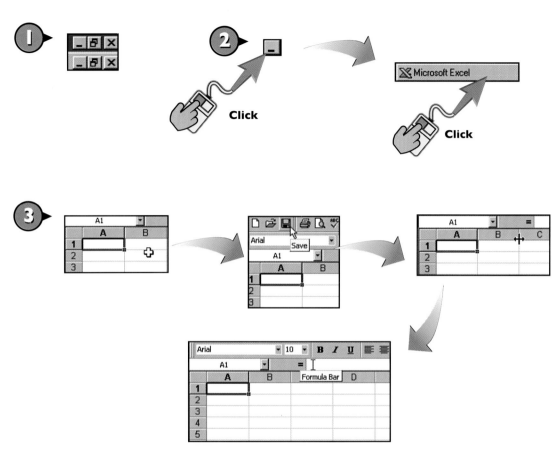

①

② Click

Microsoft Excel — Click

③

Arial — Save — A1

Arial — 10 — **B** *I* U — A1 — = | — Formula Bar

Understand the Excel Window Controls, Cursor, and Title Bar

Like the landmarks of a new neighborhood, the many features of the Excel screen become familiar in very short order. A quick tour highlights the main points of interest.

✔ **The Restore Button Changes**
The Restore button changes to a **Maximize** button after you use it to shrink the window. After you click the **Maximize** button, it reverts to the **Restore** button.

⚠ **WARNING**
If you've created work you don't want to lose, don't click the program or document Close buttons yet! Instead, see Task 10.

① Two sets of Minimize, Maximize/Restore, and Close buttons control the screen windows. The upper set controls the Excel program window; the lower set the document window.

② Click the **Minimize** button on the Excel title bar to shrink the program window to a button on the taskbar. Click the **Excel** button on the taskbar to restore the program window.

③ The mouse pointer changes shape as it changes function. Over the worksheet grid, the pointer is a white cross. At the edges of the window, it's a white arrow.

Identify Columns, Rows, and Cells

A new worksheet is like a blank sheet of paper in a notebook, ready for all the text and numbers you require. Excel's worksheets have features not found on the paper variety—after you learn these features, they'll make your work faster and easier.

✓ **Recognizing the Selected Cell**
The last cell you clicked is the selected cell. The selected cell has a border around it for easy identification. See Part 2, Tasks 1 and 2, for specific steps on selecting cells.

✓ **Excel Files are Workbooks**
Files in Excel are called workbooks, and you name and save them just as you do word processor files. You also can add worksheets to workbooks.

Task 3: Learning the Parts of the Worksheet

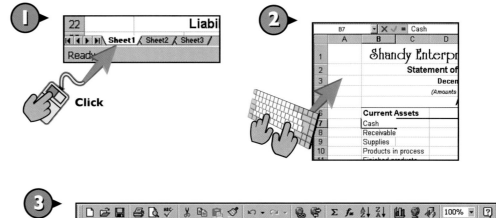

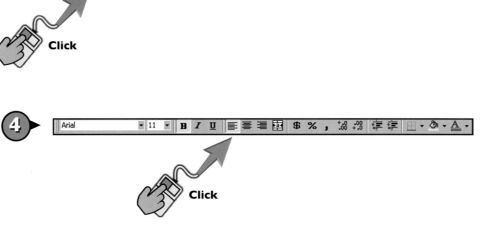

1 ▶ The whole screen is called the worksheet. Click the **sheet tabs** to switch from worksheet to worksheet.

2 ▶ The worksheet **gridlines** divide the sheet into **cells**. The cells are organized into numbered rows and lettered columns. Click any cell and start typing to enter data.

3 ▶ Click buttons on the Standard toolbar to perform standard chores such as opening files and printing.

4 ▶ Click any of the tools on the Formatting toolbar to change the appearance of text and numbers in the selected cell.

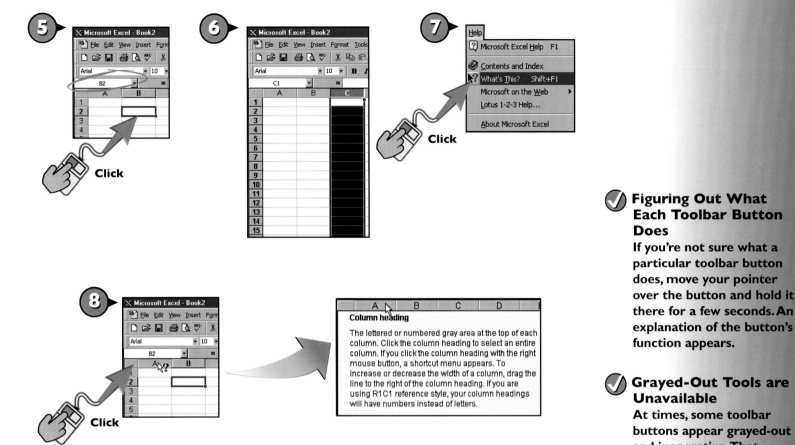

5 ▸ A **cell reference** consists of a column letter and a row number. If you click the cell in **column B**, **row 2**, the cell reference B2 appears in the worksheet's **name box**.

6 ▸ The letters at the top of each column are called **column headings**, and the numbers at the beginning of each row are called **row headings**.

7 ▸ If any feature on the worksheet presents a puzzle, choose **Help, What's This?**. The mouse pointer sprouts a question mark.

8 ▸ Then click any area of the worksheet and Excel provides a quick explanation of the puzzling item's function.

Task 4: Scrolling the Worksheet

Navigate the Excel Screen

Only a portion of the Excel worksheet is visible at any one time. You can use the *scrollbars* at the bottom and far right of the Excel screen to view other portions of the worksheet.

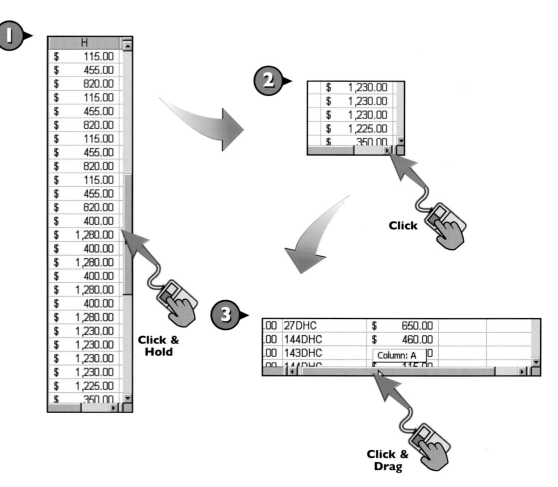

Start Here

Click

Click & Hold

Click & Drag

✓ **Scroll Many Rows or Columns at a Time**
To scroll many rows or columns at a time, point at any of the scroll buttons. Then hold down the left mouse key until you reach the desired location on the worksheet.

I Use the vertical scrollbar to move up and down in the worksheet; drag the **scroll box** to move quickly. (You can also click above or below the scroll box to move up or down one screen.)

2 Click the **scroll buttons** to scroll the view one column or row at a time.

3 As you drag a scroll box, a **ScreenTip** tells you the current worksheet location.

End Task

Task 5: Moving Around the Worksheet

Start Here

①

	A	B	C	D
1	**Boulder Quarries Inc.**			
2	**Consolidated Income Statement**			
3		*1995*	*1996*	*1997*
4				
5	**Gross Revenue**	$150,000	$150,500	$151,000
6	Cost of Goods Sold	$26,565	$26,865	$27,165
7	**Gross Profit**	$123,435	$123,635	$123,835
8	Rent	$12,000	$12,067	$12,134
9	General Administration	$2,500	$2,532	$2,564
10	Utilities	$1,000	$1,058	$1,116
11	**Expenses**	$14,500	$14,599	$14,689
12	**Operating Income**	$108,935	$109,036	$109,137
13				
14	*Date Verified*		4/13/96	3/12/97

`Ctrl`+`End`

`Ctrl`+`Home`

②

	A	B	C	D	E
1	**Boulder Quarries Inc.**				
2	**Consolidated Income Statement**				
3		*1995*	*1996*	*1997*	
4					
5	**Gross Revenue**	$150,000	$150,500	$151,000	
6	Cost of Goods Sold	$26,565	$26,865	$27,165	
7	**Gross Profit**	$123,435	$123,635	$123,835	
8	Rent	$12,000	$12,067	$12,134	
9	General Administration	$2,500	$2,532	$2,564	
10	Utilities	$1,000	$1,058	$1,116	
11	**Expenses**	$14,500	$14,599	$14,689	
12	**Operating Income**	$108,935	$109,036	$109,137	
13					
14	*Date Verified*		4/13/96	3/12/97	
15					

③

	A	B	C	D
1	**Boulder Quarries Inc.**			
2	**Consolidated Income Statement**			
3		*1995*	*1996*	*1997*
4				
5	**Gross Revenue**	$150,000	$150,500	$151,000
6	Cost of Goods Sold	$26,565	$26,865	$27,165
7	**Gross Profit**	$123,435	$123,635	$123,835

`Ctrl`+`←`

④

	A	B	C	D
1	*Customer*	*Client #*	*Part #*	*Quantity*
2	Majorca Ventures	C015	HC46	1
3	South Eaton PLC.	C012	DC29	3
4	Majorca Ventures	C015	HC46	1
5	South Eaton PLC.	C012	DC29	3
6	Majorca Ventures	C015	HC46	1
7	South Eaton PLC.	C012	DC29	3

`PgUp`

	A	B	C	D
26	Katounia Corp.	C002	HC44	1
27	Madras Trading	C010	DC27	7
28	Taylor Views Inc.	C015	HC46	2
29	Katounia Corp.	C002	HC44	1
30	Madras Trading	C010	DC27	7
31	Taylor Views Inc.	C015	HC46	2
32	Katounia Corp.	C002	HC44	1

`PgDn`

View Other Parts of the Worksheet

Scrolling across a worksheet is like moving a magnifying glass over a huge page of text. Moving the cursor around the worksheet is more like turning pages—it's how you get from place to place. To move short distances, click the desired cell or press an arrow key. For bigger moves, keyboard key combinations work best.

✓ **Use the Home Key**
The fastest way to get back to the beginning of a row (column **A**) is to press Home from any location in that row.

✓ **Moving to a Specific Cell**
To go to a specific cell in a large worksheet, type the cell reference in the name box (on the Formula bar) and press Enter.

① To move to the intersection of the last row and column that contain data (the lower-right corner of the worksheet data), press **Ctrl+End**.

② To move back to the first cell in the worksheet (cell **A1**), press **Ctrl+Home**.

③ To move to the first or last occupied cell in a row or column, press **Ctrl** and the **arrow** key that points in the direction you want to move.

④ To move up or down one screen at a time, press the **Page Up** or **Page Down** key.

End Task

Task 6: Using the Office Assistant

Get Help in Excel

All Excel users have one thing in common. At some point, we all ask, "How do I...?" The Office Assistant is designed to answer this and all your other Excel questions.

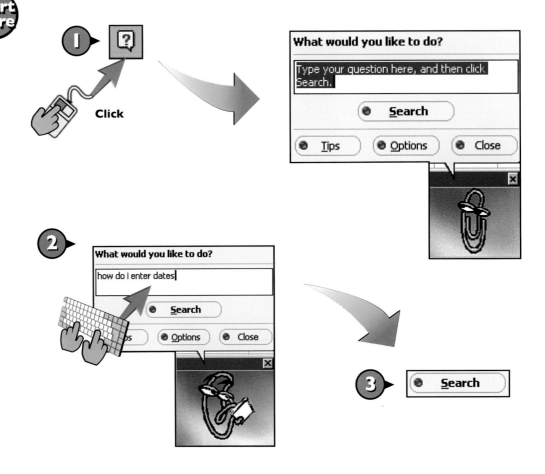

✓ Fast Searches in Help

Searches for Help are faster if your Office Assistant queries are as specific as possible. Typing "How do I enter dates," for example, gets the relevant topic faster than typing "How do I enter data?"

ⓘ WARNING

Don't click outside the Office Assistant balloon until you finish choosing your Help topic. Clicking too soon causes the balloon to disappear. To get the balloon back, click the Office Assistant.

1 ▶ Click the **Office Assistant** button on the Standard toolbar to summon the Office Assistant.

2 ▶ Type your question in the Office Assistant balloon (just type over the highlighted text). For example, type `how do I enter dates`.

3 ▶ Click **Search**.

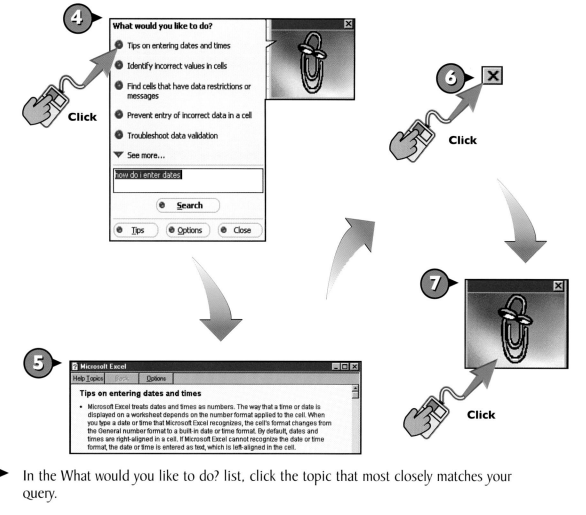

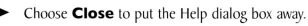

4 In the What would you like to do? list, click the topic that most closely matches your query.

5 The Microsoft Excel Help dialog box appears. Read the displayed Help topic.

6 Choose **Close** to put the Help dialog box away.

7 Choose **Close** again to close the Office Assistant window (or you can leave the Office Assistant window open for quick access).

✅ **Need a New Search?**
If none of the topics in the What Would You Like To Do? list matches your query, click See More. If you still don't see a relevant topic, try rephrasing your query and then click Search again.

✅ **Move the Assistant**
If the Office Assistant window obscures a vital section of your worksheet, click the window, hold down the left mouse button, and drag the Office Assistant out of the way.

✅ **Office Assistant Tips**
When a light bulb appears in the Office Assistant window, click it for a tip relevant to the task at hand.

Choose Office Assistant Options

Several options are available with the Office Assistant. You can have the Assistant display tips about keyboard shortcuts, you can have it display only high-priority tips, or you can activate the Tip of the Day feature.

✓ More Assistants Are Available

Depending on your Office 97 installation, you might not have all the Office Assistants on your hard disk. If that's the case, insert your Office 97 CD into the CD-ROM drive and try your Assistant change again.

✓ Office Assistants on the Web

If you have an Internet connection, you can add more choices to the Office Assistant gallery. To add more Assistants, choose Help, Microsoft on the Web, Microsoft Office Home Page.

Task 7: Changing Office Assistant Settings

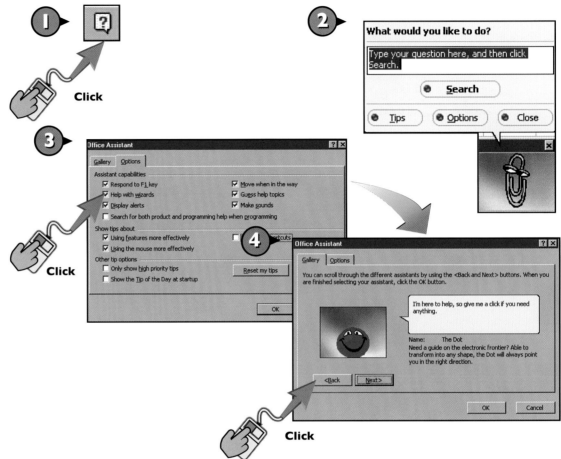

① Click the **Office Assistant** button on the Standard toolbar to summon the Office Assistant.

② Click **Options** to display the Office Assistant dialog box.

③ The Options tab lists the settings you can change. A check mark indicates a setting is active; click to turn a setting on or off. Choose **OK** to accept the changes.

④ To choose a different Office Assistant character, click the **Gallery** tab and use **Back** and **Next** to see the different Office Assistants available.

Task 8: Displaying Help Contents

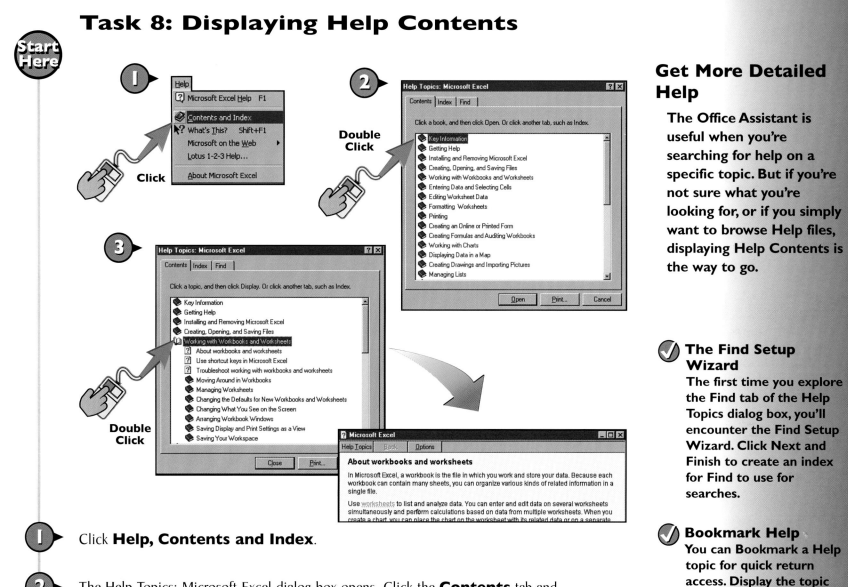

Get More Detailed Help

The Office Assistant is useful when you're searching for help on a specific topic. But if you're not sure what you're looking for, or if you simply want to browse Help files, displaying Help Contents is the way to go.

✅ **The Find Setup Wizard**
The first time you explore the Find tab of the Help Topics dialog box, you'll encounter the Find Setup Wizard. Click Next and Finish to create an index for Find to use for searches.

✅ **Bookmark Help**
You can Bookmark a Help topic for quick return access. Display the topic and choose Options, Define Bookmarks. Choose OK in the Bookmark Define dialog box.

1 ▶ Click **Help, Contents and Index**.

2 ▶ The Help Topics: Microsoft Excel dialog box opens. Click the **Contents** tab and double-click any of the topics.

3 ▶ Double-click the subtopic of your choice to display the Help file.

Use Zoom to Shrink or Enlarge Your View

Seeing a small corner of a worksheet in detail is useful. Getting a bird's-eye view of the entire worksheet is equally useful. With Excel's Zoom feature, you can do both.

✓ Fit Your Data to the Screen

To magnify your data to exactly fit the screen, select the data and click the Zoom drop-down arrow. Then choose Selection.

✓ Choose a Custom Zoom Factor

If none of the magnification factors on the Zoom drop-down list suits you, click the Zoom box on the Standard toolbar and type a number between 10 and 400. Press Enter to view the typed magnification factor.

Task 9: Changing Worksheet Magnification

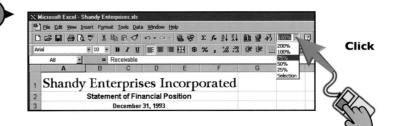

Click

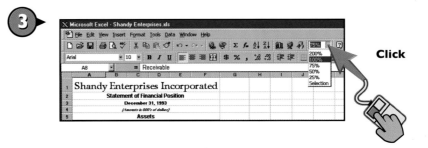

Click

 Click the **Zoom** drop-down arrow on the Standard toolbar.

2 Choose a magnification from the list—less than 100% to see more of the entire worksheet or greater than 100% to examine a corner of the worksheet in detail.

3 Click the **Zoom** drop-down arrow again and choose **100%** to return to the default worksheet magnification.

End Task

Task 10: Naming and Saving Worksheets, and Then Closing Excel

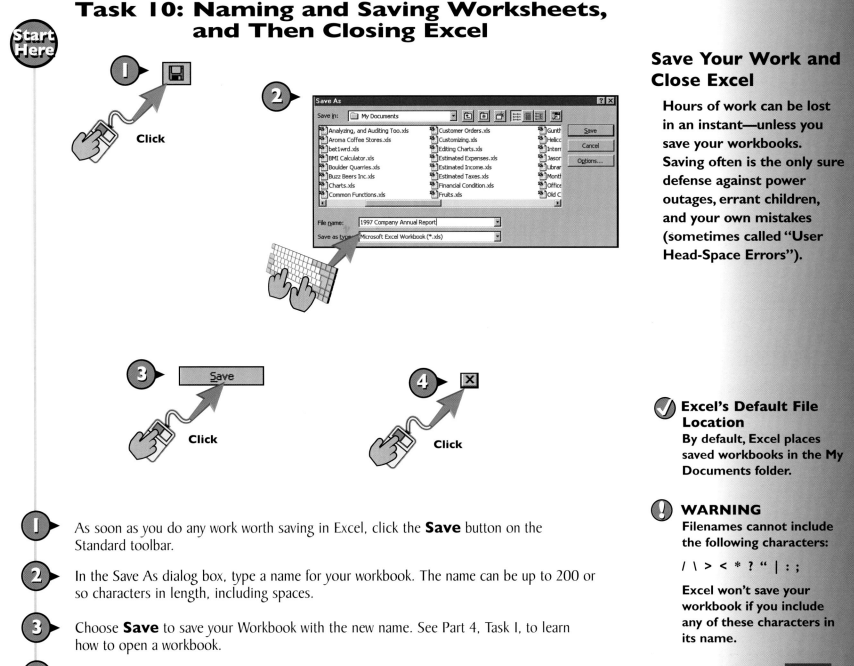

Start Here

① Click

② Save As

| File name: | 1997 Company Annual Report |
| Save as type: | Microsoft Excel Workbook (*.xls) |

③ Save — Click

④ ✕ — Click

Save Your Work and Close Excel

Hours of work can be lost in an instant—unless you save your workbooks. Saving often is the only sure defense against power outages, errant children, and your own mistakes (sometimes called "User Head-Space Errors").

✓ **Excel's Default File Location**
By default, Excel places saved workbooks in the My Documents folder.

⚠ **WARNING**
Filenames cannot include the following characters:

/ \ > < * ? " | : ;

Excel won't save your workbook if you include any of these characters in its name.

① As soon as you do any work worth saving in Excel, click the **Save** button on the Standard toolbar.

② In the Save As dialog box, type a name for your workbook. The name can be up to 200 or so characters in length, including spaces.

③ Choose **Save** to save your Workbook with the new name. See Part 4, Task 1, to learn how to open a workbook.

④ When you finish for the day, click the **Close (X)** button in the Excel title bar to exit the program.

End Task

PART 2

Entering Data

Excel is a powerful calculating engine, but like any engine, it goes nowhere without fuel. Excel's fuel is data, in the form of numbers and text.

Master a few simple techniques, and you'll find that feeding data into Excel is no more complicated than pumping gas into the family car. Part 2 looks at the basics of entering data and some data-entry tricks to save you both time and typing.

Tasks

Task 1: Selecting Cells with Keystrokes

Keyboard Cell Selection

To enter, edit, or format data in an Excel cell, you have to select the cells first. Some people prefer to use the keyboard (rather than the mouse) to select cells, because they can work faster if they leave their fingers on the keys at all times. You can decide which method you prefer—and maybe you'll use both.

✓ Quick Next-Cell Selection
Press the Tab key to select the cell to the right of the current selection. Press the Enter key to select the cell below the current selection.

✓ Expand Your Excel Vocabulary
In spreadsheets, a group of cells is referred to as a range of cells. You will see this term used in the menu commands and Help screens.

Start Here

1 Use the up-, down-, left-, and right-arrow keys to move to the cell in which you want to work.

2 To select a group of cells, select the first cell in the group. Then hold down the **Shift** key and press an **arrow** key in the desired direction to highlight cells.

3 To select a group of cells within a column, select the first cell containing data in that column and press **Shift+Ctrl+down-arrow**.

4 To select a group of cells within a row, select the first cell containing data in that row and press **Shift+Ctrl+right-arrow**.

End Task

Task 2: Selecting Cells with the Mouse

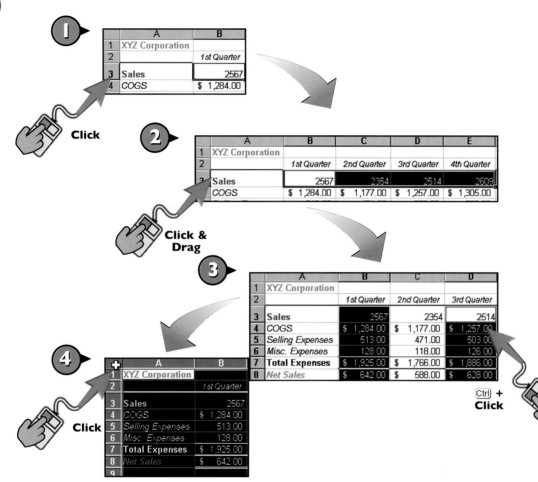

Start Here

Mouse Cell Selection

Clicking a cell to select it is pretty easy. **Dragging through multiple cells to select a range isn't much more difficult, especially if you are already using the mouse.**

✓ **Click Headings for Fast Row or Column Selection**
You can select an entire column by clicking the column heading. Click a row heading to select an entire row.

✓ **Dragging Alternative**
Unless you're very dexterous, the Shift+arrow key combination is sometimes easier than dragging through a range or group of cells.

⚠ **WARNING**
The Select All button is a useful but potentially dangerous feature. Use it with care.

1 ▶ To select a single cell, click the cell.

2 ▶ To select a range (or group) of cells for formatting or editing, click the first cell in the range, hold down the left mouse button, and drag to the end of the range.

3 ▶ To select nonadjacent cells or ranges, click to select the first cell or range. Then hold down the **Ctrl** key while you click to select additional cells or ranges.

4 ▶ To select all of the cells in the worksheet, click the **Select All** button (at the intersection of the column and row headings).

End Task

Task 3: Typing Numbers in Cells

Enter Numbers

Excel is like a word processor for numbers. Just type the numbers in selected cells, and Excel can manipulate them any way you choose. Numbers are displayed aligned to the right of the cell by default, so decimals and commas line up.

✓ **Learning More About Formatting Numbers**
See Part 5, "Formatting Worksheets," for complete information on formatting numbers.

✓ **Scientific Notation Decoded**
Whenever you type a number that cannot be fully displayed in a cell, Excel shows it in *scientific notation.* You see the first part of the number displayed, and then an E, followed by a plus symbol and the number of digits that cannot be displayed (including two decimals).

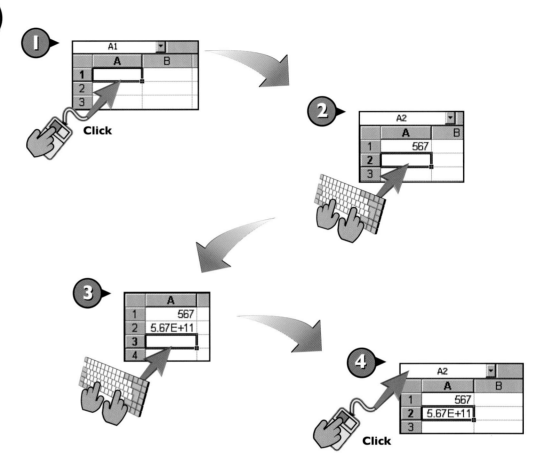

Start Here

Click

Click

1 ▶ To enter a number in a cell, you must first select the cell. For example, click cell **A1** to select it.

2 ▶ Type the number you want displayed in the cell (such as **567**) and press **Enter**. The number is placed in the cell, and the active cell moves down one row.

3 ▶ Type **567000000000** in a cell and press **Enter**.

4 ▶ Although the number appears in the Formula bar as typed, the number in the cell is in scientific notation. Click the cell to display the entire number.

Next Step

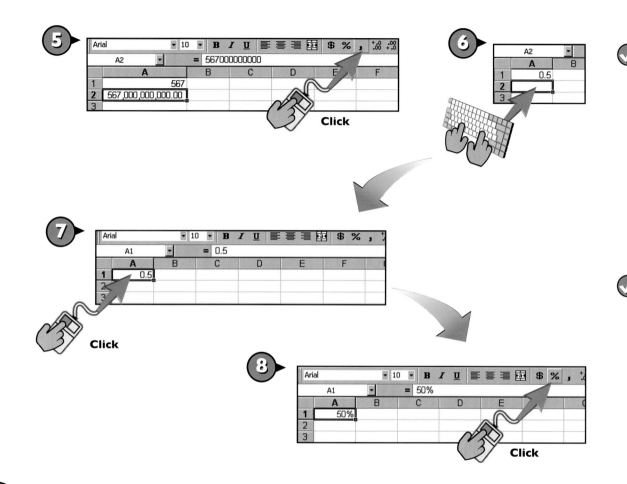

⑤ Click the **Comma Style** button on the Formatting toolbar. The column automatically widens and displays the number with commas.

⑥ To display numbers with a percent symbol, first type a number or fraction. For example, to display 50%, type **0.5** and press **Enter**.

⑦ Click the cell in which you want a percent symbol to display.

⑧ Click the **Percent Style** button on the Formatting toolbar.

✅ **Displaying Numbers with Commas**
To speed up typing numbers, don't bother typing commas (for example, just type 3000 instead of 3,000). After you type all the numbers, select the cells you want to format with a comma and click the Comma Style button on the Formatting toolbar.

✅ **Displaying Numbers with a Percent Symbol**
You can enter percents in a worksheet two ways. Type the numbers, using decimals (for example, 0.5), and then select the cells and format them as percents with the Percent Style button. Or follow each number by the % symbol as you type (for example, 50%).

⚠ **WARNING**
Be sure not to type 50 and click the Percent Style key if you mean to enter 50%—you will get 5000%. To display 50%, you must type .5 in the cell.

Task 4: Typing Text in Cells

Type Text

Although Excel looks nothing like a word processor, each cell on a worksheet behaves a little as it would in a word processor. For example, you can use the **Backspace** and **Delete** keys to edit text in Excel, just as you do in a word processor, which makes entering text a straightforward job.

✓ **Changing the Way the Enter Key Behaves**
By default, pressing Enter moves the active cell down in the worksheet. To have the Enter key move the active cell in another direction (for example, to the right), choose **Tools, Options** and click the **Edit** tab. In the Move Selection After Enter option, choose a direction from the drop-down list and click **OK**.

✓ **Other Formatting Information**
For complete information about adjusting column width, see Task 7.

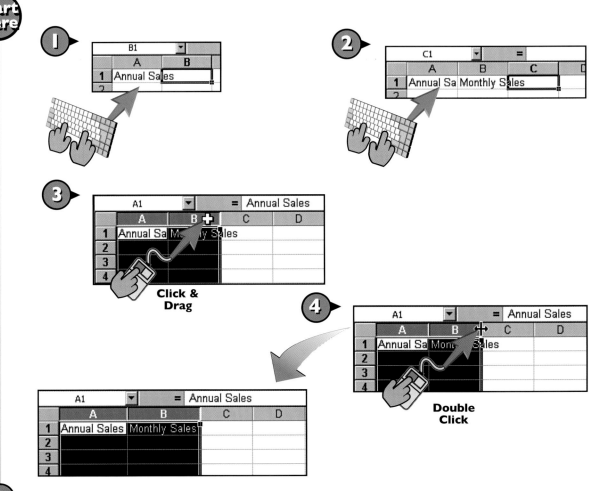

Start Here

① Click & Drag

④ Double Click

① As you type, you can use the **Delete** and **Backspace** keys to correct errors. To accept your entry, press **Enter** or **Tab**.

② Text that's longer than the width of a cell is displayed in adjacent cells if they are empty; if the adjacent cells hold data, the long text is truncated (chopped off) in the display.

③ To widen columns to display all of the text, select the column headings of the columns you want to widen. In this example, the column A and B headings are selected.

④ Position the mouse pointer on the right border of any one of the selected columns. Then double-click to widen the columns to fit the longest entry.

End Task

Task 5: Entering Text with AutoComplete

Start Here

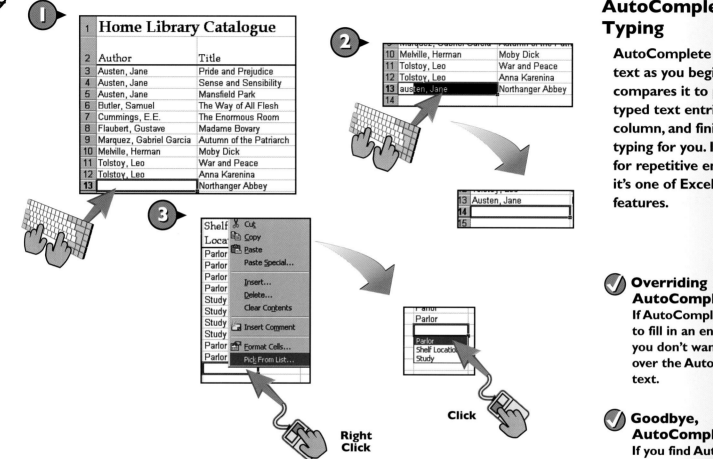

AutoComplete Saves Typing

AutoComplete looks at text as you begin to type it, compares it to previously typed text entries in the column, and finishes the typing for you. It works only for repetitive entries, but it's one of Excel's handiest features.

✓ **Overriding AutoComplete**
If AutoComplete attempts to fill in an entry with text you don't want, simply type over the AutoComplete text.

✓ **Goodbye, AutoComplete**
If you find AutoComplete more annoying than handy, turn it off. Choose **Tools, Options** and click the **Edit** tab of the Options dialog box. Click the check mark next to **Enable AutoComplete for Cell Values**, and then click **OK**.

Right Click

Click

① Type text entries in a column.

② Type the first few characters of an entry you previously typed; Excel completes the entry for you. When you press **Enter**, the completed entry is displayed.

③ To choose from a list of entries, right-click a cell. Choose **Pick From List** on the shortcut menu and choose an entry from the drop-down list.

End Task

Task 6: Correcting Data Entries

Quick Cell Edits

In Excel, data-entry mistakes, whether text or numeric, are as fixable as they are inevitable.

✓ **Two Selection Techniques**
To select text while editing inside a cell, press **Shift+Arrow**. Or simply click and drag across the text.

✓ **Escape!**
To back out of a cell without saving your editing changes, press **Esc** while the cursor is still in the cell.

⊘ **WARNING**
Don't select a cell with data in it and begin typing unless you intend to replace all of the cell contents. Typing in the active cell overwrites any existing data.

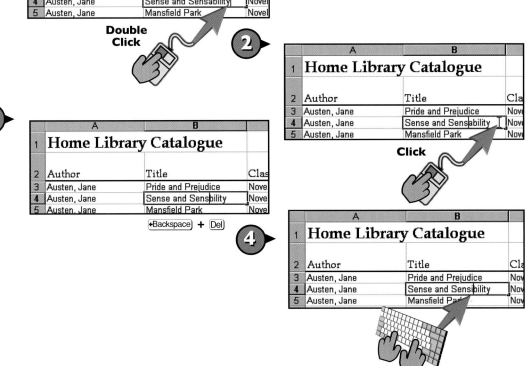

Start Here

Double Click

Click

+Backspace + Del

① Double-click the cell you want to edit. A flashing cursor appears in the cell and the mouse pointer is an I-beam.

② Click with the mouse to position the cursor if you want to edit just a few characters.

③ Press **Backspace** to delete characters to the left of the cursor. Press **Del** to delete to the right of the cursor.

④ Type any new text and press **Enter** to save the changes.

End Task

Task 7: Adjusting Column Width

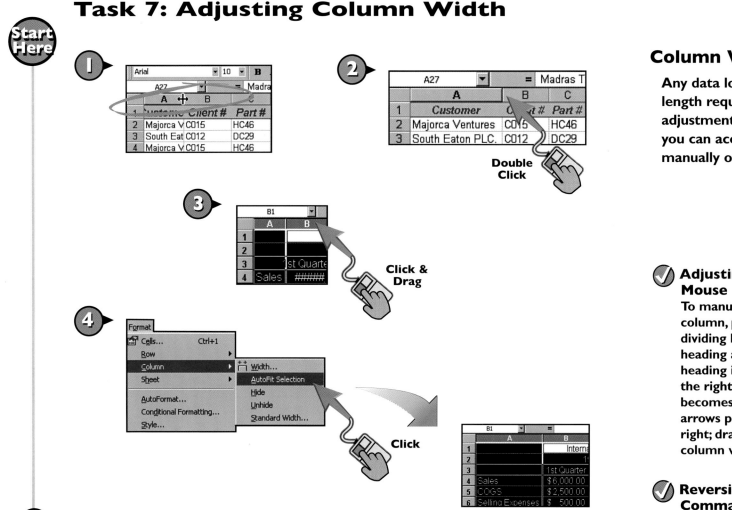

Column Width

Any data longer than a cell length requires column adjustment—a quick chore you can accomplish manually or automatically.

Double Click

Click & Drag

Click

✓ **Adjusting with the Mouse**

To manually adjust a column, point at the dividing line between its heading and the column heading immediately to the right. The pointer becomes a plus sign with arrows pointing left and right; drag to change the column width.

✓ **Reversing the AutoFit Command**

If **AutoFit** has made your columns wider than you want them, click the **Undo** button on the Standard toolbar to reverse the adjustment. Adjust the column widths manually to the desired width.

1 To adjust the width of a single column, point at the line dividing its heading from the column heading immediately to the right.

2 Double-click the dividing line between the column headings. The column width automatically adjusts to the longest data in the column.

3 To adjust the width of two or more adjacent columns, click and drag across the column headings.

4 Choose **Format, Column, AutoFit Selection**. The columns are fitted to the widest data.

End Task

Task 8: Adjusting Row Height

Change Row Height

Just as with column width, row height is adjusted either automatically or manually. The occasion for it arises less frequently, however.

Start Here

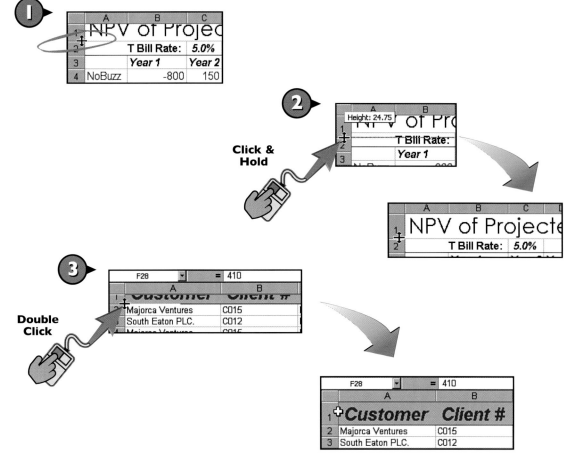

Click & Hold

Double Click

Height Adjustments Affect the Entire Row
You can't adjust the height of a single cell in a row. Only height adjustments for an entire row are possible.

Enlarging Fonts
Whenever you enlarge the font size of data in a row, the row height automatically adjusts.

I To adjust the height of a single row, point at the dividing line between its heading and the row heading below. The pointer becomes a plus sign with arrows pointing up and down.

2 Hold down the left mouse button and drag the double-headed arrow up or down to adjust the row height. A **ScreenTip** displays the height as you drag the mouse.

3 For automatic height adjustments, double-click the dividing line between a row heading and the row immediately below it. The entire row is fitted to the tallest data in the row.

End Task

Task 9: Entering Dates and Times

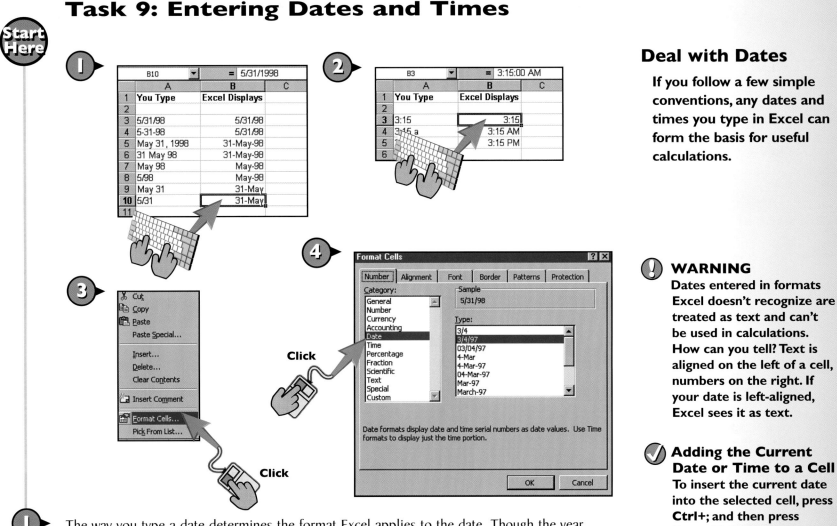

Deal with Dates

If you follow a few simple conventions, any dates and times you type in Excel can form the basis for useful calculations.

⚠ WARNING

Dates entered in formats Excel doesn't recognize are treated as text and can't be used in calculations. How can you tell? Text is aligned on the left of a cell, numbers on the right. If your date is left-aligned, Excel sees it as text.

✔ Adding the Current Date or Time to a Cell

To insert the current date into the selected cell, press **Ctrl+;** and then press **Enter.** To insert the current time into the selected cell, press **Ctrl+Shift+;** and press **Enter.** The date and time come from your computer's internal clock.

---

1 ► The way you type a date determines the format Excel applies to the date. Though the year was not entered in cells, the Formula bar shows the current year (1998).

2 ► Excel records time using a 24-hour clock. To specify AM or PM, type the time, followed by a space and either **a** (for AM) or **p** (for PM). Then press **Enter**.

3 ► Use a *shortcut menu* to apply one of Excel's other date or time formats to a cell; after you right-click the cell, choose **Format Cells** on the shortcut menu.

4 ► Click the **Number** tab of the Format Cells dialog box; then choose either **Date** or **Time** from the Category list. Choose a format from the Type list and click **OK**.

Task 10: Entering Data with AutoFill

AutoFill Speeds Data Entry

Instead of typing out the names of all months, days, or quarters of the year, just type the first entry in the series. AutoFill will fill in the rest for you!

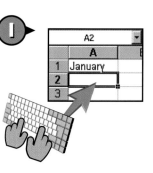

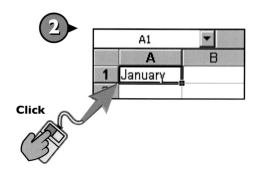

Click

Click

✓ Complete a Series in Any Direction

AutoFill works in any direction. Drag the fill handle up, down, left, or right, and Excel completes the series in the chosen direction.

✓ Filling a Series of Numbers

See Task 11 for information on automatically completing a numeric series, such as sequential numbers or dates.

 Type the starting entry in a series and press **Enter**. Examples might be January, Monday, or Qtr 1.

 Click the cell containing the entry, and position the pointer over the selected cell's *fill handle*. The pointer becomes a black cross.

 Drag the fill handle through the cells next to or below the selected cell. A ScreenTip displays each increment as you drag.

Release the mouse button, and the series fills the selected cells.

Next Step

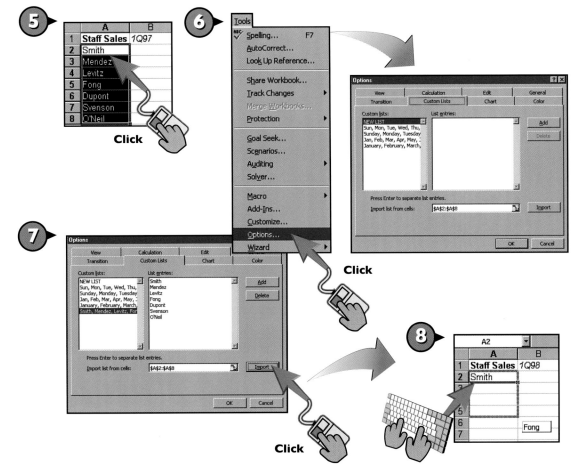

WARNING
Don't drag the fill handle through cells that already hold data unless you intend to overwrite these cells.

Numbers as Part of Text Entries
AutoFill can increment numbers even when they are surrounded by text. For example, type Patient 1, Medical Records. Then drag the fill handle and the series continues as Patient 2, Medical Records, and so on.

Start Anywhere in the Series
You can start the sequence with any entry in the series, for example, April. The cells fill as you drag the fill handle. When you reach the end of the series (December), the cells continue to fill, starting with the beginning of the series (January).

5 To create a custom list for a series you must type often, type the entire series and select it.

6 Choose **Tools, Options**. The Options dialog box opens. Click the **Custom Lists** tab.

7 Choose **Import** and then choose **OK**.

8 The next time you want to use this series, type the first entry and then drag the fill handle to complete the series (as in steps 1–4).

End Task

Numbered Series

Completing a numbered series is a simple dragging operation in Excel, even for growth series and trend lines.

✓ Filling Growth and Trend Series

For growth series and trends, follow steps 1–3 of Task 11. Choose **Series** on the shortcut menu, make your choices in the Series dialog box, and click **OK**.

✓ Copying Numbers

If you drag the fill handle of a cell while holding a number with the left mouse button, the number is copied to the selected cells.

✓ Creating Nonsequential Numbers

For a series that increments by a number other than one, type the first two or more numbers in the series. Select all the cells holding the data. Drag the fill handle of the last cell with data, using the left mouse button.

Task 11: Entering a Series

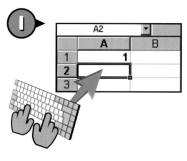

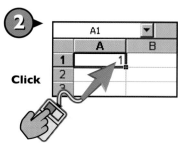

Click

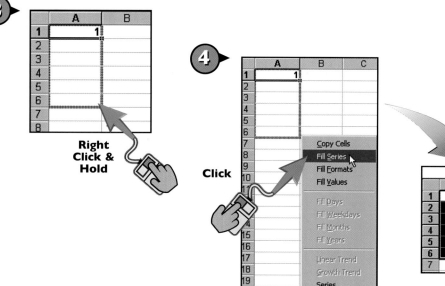

Right Click & Hold

Click

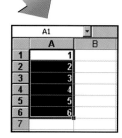

Copy Cells
Fill Series
Fill Formats
Fill Values

Fill Days
Fill Weekdays
Fill Months
Fill Years

Linear Trend
Growth Trend

Series...

Type the first number in the series and press **Enter**.

Click the cell containing the data and position the pointer over the cell's fill handle.

Click and hold the right mouse button. The pointer turns into a white arrow. Drag the white arrow through the desired number of cells.

Choose **Fill Series** on the shortcut menu, and the series fills the selected cells.

Task 12: Inserting Special Characters

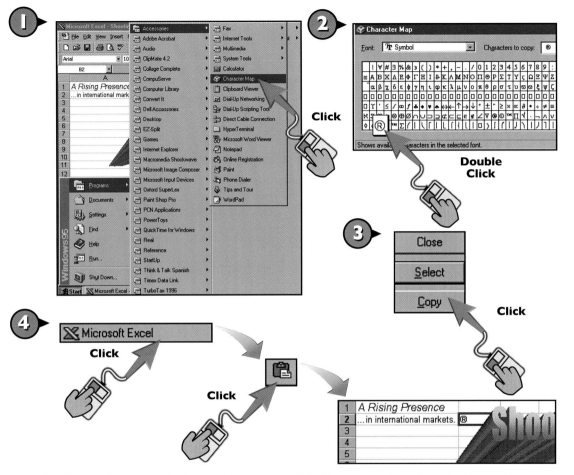

Click

Double Click

Click

Click

Click

Click

Enter ®, ™, and Other Symbols

When the need arises for special characters in your worksheets, they're available—although you go outside Excel to find them. As with most cell-editing functions, you must select the cell before you can add a special character to it.

⊘ WARNING

To insert a special character in the middle of an existing cell entry, you must first double-click to edit the entry and place the flashing cursor at the position where you want the special character. Otherwise, the special character replaces the existing entry.

✓ You Don't Have to Insert Currency Symbols

To format currency with yen, pounds sterling, and other foreign symbols, see Part 5, Task 1.

---

1 With the destination cell selected, click the **Start** button on the Windows taskbar and choose **Programs, Accessories, Character Map**.

2 Double-click the special character you need in the Character Map dialog box. The character is displayed in the Characters to Copy box.

3 Choose **Copy** to place the symbol on the Clipboard; then choose **Close** to close the Character Map dialog box.

4 Click the **Microsoft Excel** button on the taskbar to return to Excel. Click the **Paste** button on the Standard toolbar to paste the symbol into the selected worksheet cell.

End Task

Editing Data

Entering data in Excel is usually just a first step. After the numbers and text are entered, they change constantly. Data needs to be corrected, moved around, deleted, and added.

Excel worksheets are designed to handle such changes with ease. Part 3 looks at the various ways you can perfect worksheets through editing.

Tasks

Task 1: Copying and Pasting Cells

Copying Cells and Their Contents

Copy and paste, the Windows standby, is often the best way to save time and typing of repetitive data in Excel.

✓ **Drag-and-Drop Method of Copying**
An alternative method for copying and pasting: select the cell or cells to be copied. Point at the border of the selected cell or cells. The pointer should be a white arrow. Hold down the **Ctrl** key, hold down the left mouse button, and drag to the destination cell.

✓ **Copying Data to Adjacent Cells**
To copy cells with the fill handle, see Task 3.

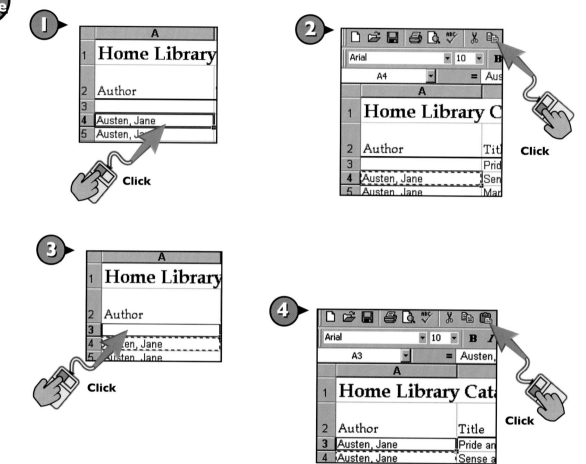

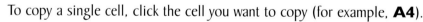

1 To copy a single cell, click the cell you want to copy (for example, **A4**).

2 Click the **Copy** button on the Standard toolbar. A moving border or **marquee** appears around the selected cell.

3 Click the destination cell where you want the copy to be pasted (for example, **A3**).

4 Click the **Paste** button on the Standard toolbar. The copied data appears in the destination cell.

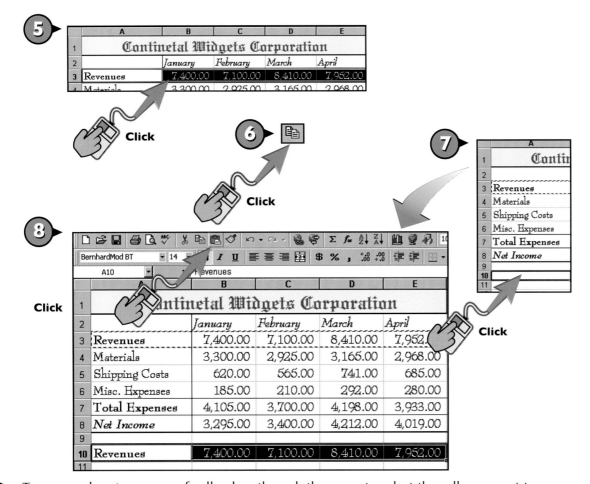

Click

Click

Click

Click

✓ **Copying to Different Locations**
To make multiple copies, click another destination cell and then click the **Paste** button on the Standard toolbar again.

✓ **Backing Out**
To cancel a copy operation before you paste anything, press **Esc.** The marquee disappears from the original cell.

⑤ To copy and paste a range of cells, drag through the range to select the cells you want to copy (for example, **A3–E3**).

⑥ Click the **Copy** button on the Standard toolbar.

⑦ Click the cell you intend to be the upper-left corner of the pasted range (for example, **A10**).

⑧ Click the **Paste** button on the Standard toolbar. The range of cells is copied in the new location.

End
Task

Cutting and Pasting Without Glue

Often you need to move data from its original location in the worksheet. When cells have to be taken from one place on the worksheet and pasted in another, the quickest way of moving them is to use cut and paste.

 Keyboard Shortcut
Instead of using the mouse, press **Ctrl+X** to cut and **Ctrl+V** to paste.

WARNING
If you select an entire destination range instead of selecting only the cell at the upper-left corner of the destination range, you get an error message from Excel unless the destination range is the exact size and shape of the original range.

Task 2: Cutting and Pasting Cells

 Start Here

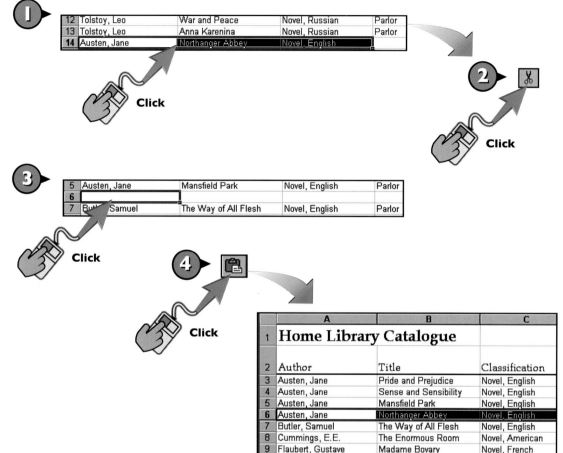

12	Tolstoy, Leo	War and Peace	Novel, Russian	Parlor
13	Tolstoy, Leo	Anna Karenina	Novel, Russian	Parlor
14	Austen, Jane	Northanger Abbey	Novel, English	

Click

Click

5	Austen, Jane	Mansfield Park	Novel, English	Parlor
6				
7	Butler, Samuel	The Way of All Flesh	Novel, English	Parlor

Click

Click

	A	B	C
1	Home Library Catalogue		
2	Author	Title	Classification
3	Austen, Jane	Pride and Prejudice	Novel, English
4	Austen, Jane	Sense and Sensibility	Novel, English
5	Austen, Jane	Mansfield Park	Novel, English
6	Austen, Jane	Northanger Abbey	Novel, English
7	Butler, Samuel	The Way of All Flesh	Novel, English
8	Cummings, E.E.	The Enormous Room	Novel, American
9	Flaubert, Gustave	Madame Bovary	Novel, French

1 Select the cell or cells to be cut (for example, **A14–C14**).

2 Click the **Cut** button on the Standard toolbar.

3 Click the destination cell (for example, **A6**). If you are moving a range of cells, select the cell in the upper-left corner of the destination range.

4 Click the **Paste** button on the Standard toolbar. The cell or range of cells is moved to the destination.

 End Task

Task 3: Copying Data Across Rows and Down Columns

Start Here

1

3		1st Quarter		2nd Quarter		3rd Quarter		4th Quarter
4	Sales	$	6,000	$	6,900	$	7,935	$ 9,125
5	COGS		2,500		2,875		3,306	3,802
6	Selling Expenses		500		575		661	760
7	Misc. Expenses		200					

Click

2

	500
	200
$	3,200

3

es	500	575	661	760
s	200			
es	$ 3,200	$ 3,450	$ 3,968	$ 0 3

Click & Hold

4

3		1st Quarter		2nd Quarter		3rd Quarter		4th Quarter
4	Sales	$	6,000	$	6,900	$	7,935	$ 9,125
5	COGS		2,500		2,875		3,306	3,802
6	Selling Expenses		500		575		661	760
7	Misc. Expenses		200		200		200	200
8	Total Expenses	$	3,200	$	3,650	$	4,168	$ 4,763

1 Select the cell to be copied.

2 Point at the fill handle in the lower-right corner of the selected cell. The pointer becomes a black cross.

3 Hold down the left mouse button and drag across the row or down the column where you want to place copies.

4 Release the mouse button. The copied cell fills the selected row or column.

Automatic Copying in Excel

A quick drag operation is all that's required to make multiple cell copies across rows or down columns. For example, suppose you pay a monthly rent of $500. Rather than typing in $500 for each month's rent, you can copy the amount. This technique only works if the destination cells are in adjacent rows or columns.

✓ Copying a Range of Cells
To copy a range with the **fill handle**, select the range first. Then drag the fill handle of the bottom or right-most cell.

✓ Copying Sequential Numbers
To copy a numeric series without incrementing it, select the series and drag the fill handle of the bottom or right-most cell with the right mouse button. Then choose **Copy Cells** on the shortcut menu.

Task 4: Moving Cells

Moving Cells Around the Worksheet

When the data in a cell has to be moved across a short stretch of worksheet, dragging is the fastest method.

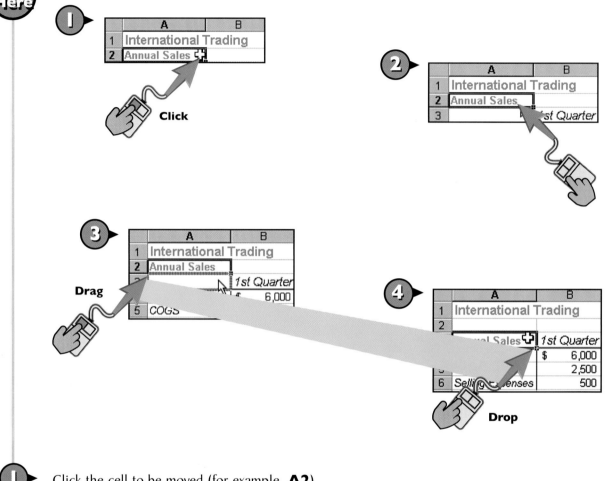

Start Here

Click

Drag

Drop

 Can't See the Destination Cell?
For moves across long stretches of worksheet, especially when the destination cell is out of view, try cutting and pasting instead of dragging (see Task 2).

⚠ WARNING
If the destination cell contains data, it will be overwritten by the moved cell.

1 Click the cell to be moved (for example, **A2**).

2 Point at the border of the selected cell. The mouse pointer should be a white arrow.

3 Hold down the left mouse button and drag the selected cell to the destination cell (for example, **A3**).

4 Release the mouse button to complete the move.

 End Task

Task 5: Moving Ranges of Cells

Start Here

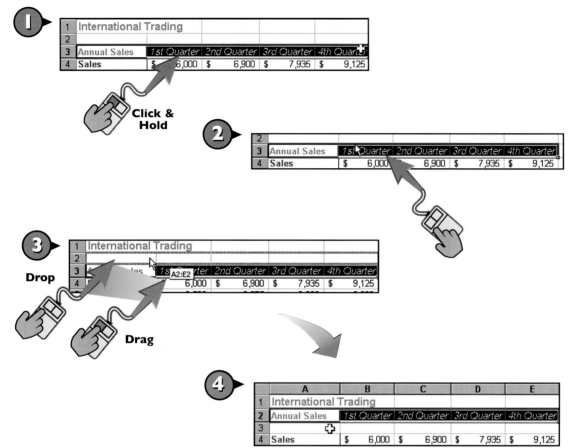

Moving Blocks of Cells

Moving the data in a range is just like moving the data in a single cell; select, drag, and drop.

✓ **The Keyboard Might Be Easier**
It's sometimes easier to select a range with a keyboard shortcut instead of by dragging. Select the first cell in the range and hold the **Shift** key down. Then use the arrow keys to select additional cells.

✓ **Dragging with the Right Mouse Button**
If you drag a selected cell or range with the right mouse button, a shortcut menu pops up when you release the mouse button. Take your choice of copying or moving the cells.

1 ▶ Drag through the range to select the cells to be moved (for example, **A3—E3**).

2 ▶ Point at the border of the selected range. The pointer should be a white arrow.

3 ▶ Hold down the left mouse button and drag the selected range to the cell at the upper-left corner of the destination range (for example, **A2**).

4 ▶ Release the mouse button to complete the move.

Task 6: Inserting Columns and Rows

Adding Workspace with Extra Rows and Columns

No matter how many columns or rows you think you'll need at the outset, you'll likely want more. Adding rows and columns, even in the middle of a full worksheet, is a quick job. New columns are inserted to the left of the selected column; new rows are inserted above the selected row.

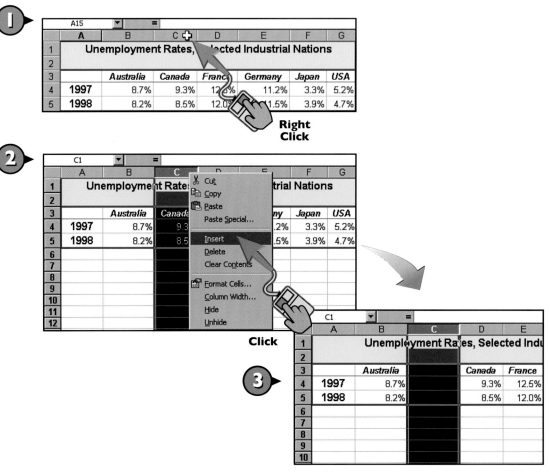

✔ **Inserting Multiple Columns or Rows**

To insert two or more columns or rows, drag across the number of row or column headings equal to the number you want to insert. Right-click any selected heading and choose Insert on the shortcut menu. Excel inserts a row or column for each row or column you selected.

① To insert a new column, right-click the column heading where you want the new column to appear.

② Choose **Insert** on the shortcut menu.

③ The new column is inserted to the left of the selected column. (The new row is inserted above the selected row.)

Task 7: Inserting Cells

1

	A	B	C
3	**Boulder Quarries Inc.**		
4	Consolidated Incor Statement		
5		*1995*	*1996*
6			
7	**Gross Revenue**	$150,000	$150,500
8	Cost of Goods Sold	$26,565	$26,865
9	**Gross Profit**	435	$123,635
10	Rent	00	$12,067
11	General Administrative	000	$2,532
12	Utilities	$1,000	$1,058

Right Click

2

Cut
Copy
Paste
Paste Special...

Insert...
Delete...
Clear Contents

Insert Comment

Format Cells...
Pick From List...

Click

3

Insert

Insert
- Shift cells right
- Shift cells down
- Entire row
- Entire column

OK
Cancel

Click

	A	B	C
3	**Boulder Quarries Inc.**		
4		Consolidated Income Statem	
5		*1995*	*1996*
6	**Gross Revenue**	$150,000	$150,500
7	Cost of Goods Sold	$26,565	$26,865

Adding Cells to Worksheets

Inserting a few extra cells in your worksheet is a simple matter of deciding where to put them. When you insert a new cell, you have the option of "shifting" existing cells down or to the right to make room for the new cell.

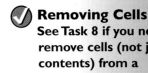 **Inserting Multiple Cells**

To insert two or more new cells, select a range of cells equal to the number of new cells you want to insert and in the exact position where you want them inserted.

✓ **Removing Cells**

See Task 8 if you need to remove cells (not just their contents) from a worksheet.

1 Right-click the cell where you want the new cell to be inserted (for example, cell **A4**).

2 Choose **Insert** on the shortcut menu.

3 In the Insert dialog box, choose **Shift Cells Down**. Choose **Shift Cells Right** to insert a cell and move the data. Then click **OK**.

End Task

Task 8: Deleting Cells

Deleting Cells

When you delete a cell, you are not just removing the contents of the cell—you are removing the cell itself. You have the option of "shifting" the remaining cells up or to the left to fill the void left by removing the cell.

See Task 9 if you want to delete only the cell contents.

Start Here

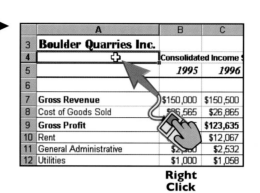

Right Click

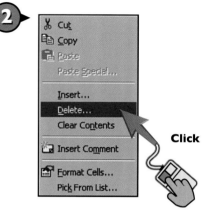

Click

✓ **To Remove Multiple Cells**

To delete more than one cell, select the entire range to be deleted before you right-click.

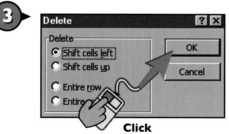

Click

⊘ **WARNING**

Be sure to point at cells or ranges with the white cross before right-clicking for the context menu. Pointing at a cell or range border with the white arrow won't produce the shortcut menu.

Right-click the cell you want to delete.

Choose **Delete** on the shortcut menu.

In the Delete dialog box, choose **Shift Cells Left** or **Shift Cells Up** and click **OK**. The cell is deleted and the remaining cells shift left or up to fill the space previously occupied.

End Task

Task 9: Deleting Cell Contents

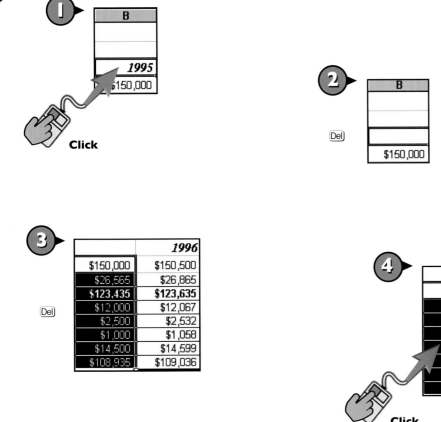

Click

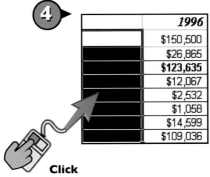

Del

Wiping Cells Clear

Deleting the contents of a cell is like wiping a blackboard. The existing cell stays in place, but its contents vanish.

Del

Click

 Click the cell whose contents you want to delete.

② Press the **Delete** key.

③ To delete multiple cell contents, click and drag to select a range of cells.

④ Press the **Delete** key.

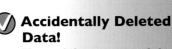 **Accidentally Deleted Data!**

If you delete any work by accident, immediately press **Ctrl+Z** to undo the deletion. See Task 15 for more information on undoing your edits.

End Task

Task 10: Deleting Columns and Rows

Removing Columns, Rows, and Their Contents

Deleting columns and rows in Excel eliminates both the cell contents and the cells themselves. Use this procedure when you want to remove an entire set of data but don't want to be left with a blank column or row where the data was in your worksheet.

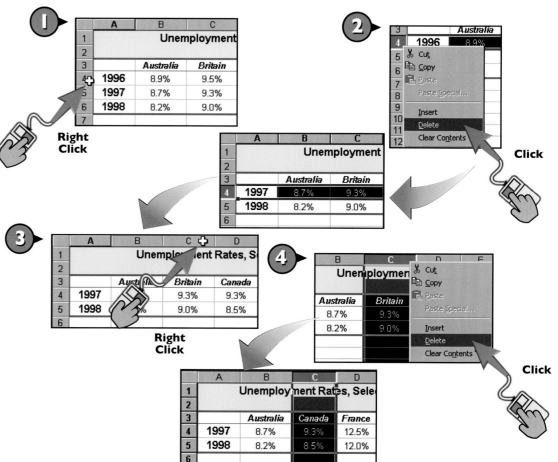

✓ **Deleting Cell Contents Only**
See Task 9 to learn how to delete the contents of an entire row or column, leaving the empty cells in place.

✓ **What Happens When You Delete**
Deleting a column moves the remaining columns to the left. Deleting a row moves the existing rows up.

1 To delete a row, right-click the row heading.

2 Click **Delete** on the shortcut menu. The row is deleted and the remaining rows move up.

3 To delete a column, right-click the column heading.

4 Click **Delete** on the shortcut menu; the column is deleted and the remaining columns move to the left.

Task 11: Moving Columns and Rows

Start Here

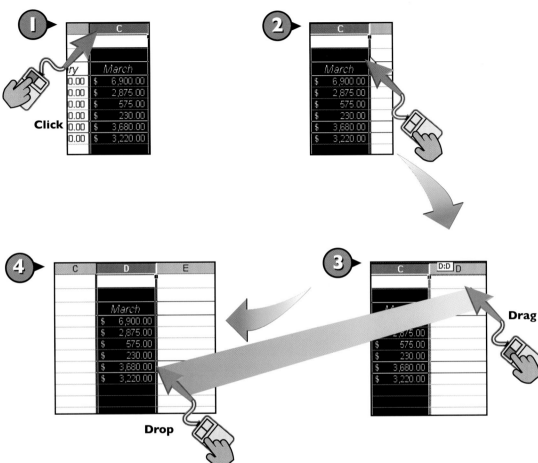

Click

Drag

Drop

Rearranging Data

No worksheet is carved in stone. Everything on the sheet can be rearranged, including entire columns and rows.

✓ **Undo the Move**
If you accidentally move the data into the wrong area, you can undo the move by immediately pressing **Ctrl+Z**. See Task 15 for more information.

⚠ **WARNING**
Moving rows or columns to locations with existing content will overwrite that content. To avoid overwriting existing cells, insert a blank row or column first. Then move the row or column into the newly added blank area.

1. ➤ Click the row or column heading for the row or column you wish to move. To select multiple rows or columns, drag through the desired headings.

2. ➤ Point at the row or column border; the mouse pointer changes to a white arrow.

3. ➤ Hold down the left mouse button and drag the row or column to the desired location. An outline of the selected row or column indicates the destination as you drag.

4. ➤ Release the mouse button to drop the column or row into its new location.

End Task

Task 12: Editing Inside the Cell

Tips for Cell Edits

You'll sometimes find it necessary to change part of the data in a cell. Instead of retyping the entire cell contents, you can easily change a single character or word in a cell, using the standard editing keys you're familiar with from Microsoft Word.

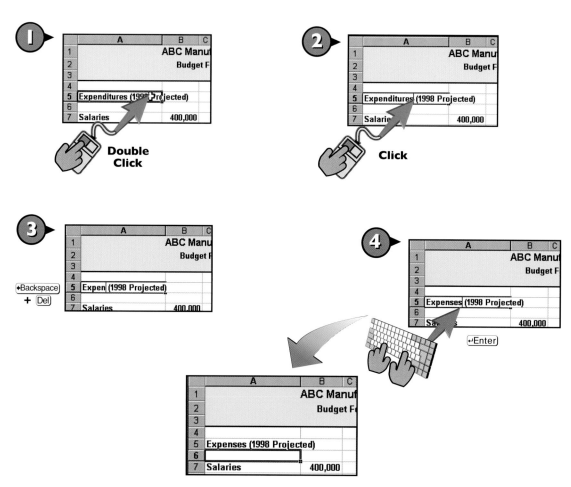

✓ Moving and Copying Part of a Cell

You can move or copy part of a cell. Select the specific data and click the **Cut** button to move or the **Copy** button to copy. Double-click the destination cell and click inside the cell where you want the data to go; then choose the **Paste** button.

 Double-click the cell to be edited.

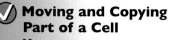 Click to position your cursor next to the characters you want to edit.

Press the **Backspace** key to remove a character to the left of the flashing cursor. Press **Delete** to remove a character to the right of the flashing cursor.

Type any corrections and press **Enter** to save your editing changes.

End Task

Task 13: Checking Spelling

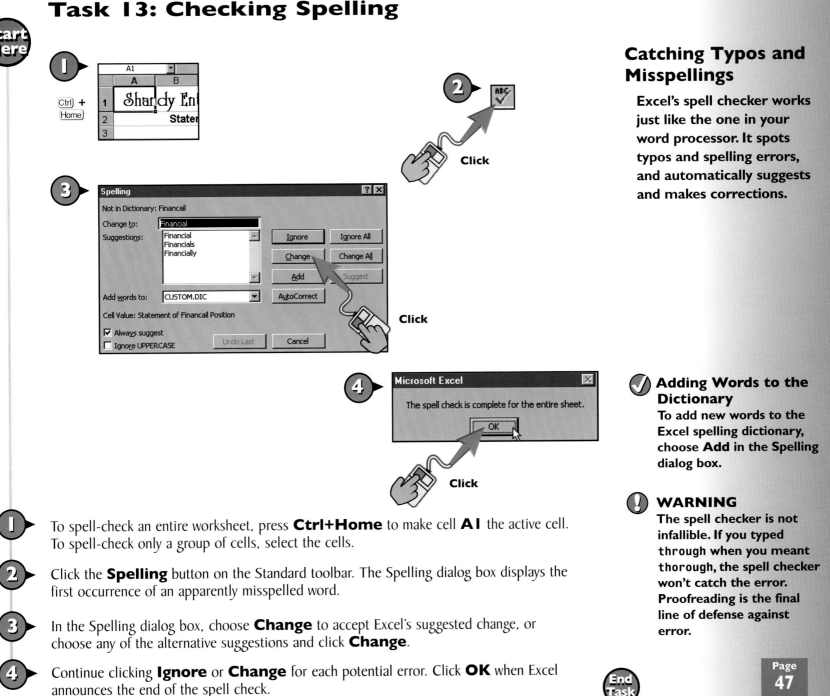

Catching Typos and Misspellings

Excel's spell checker works just like the one in your word processor. It spots typos and spelling errors, and automatically suggests and makes corrections.

Spelling dialog box details:

Not in Dictionary: Financail

Change to: Financial

Suggestions:
Financial
Financials
Financially

Add words to: CUSTOM.DIC

Cell Value: Statement of Financail Position

☑ Always suggest
☐ Ignore UPPERCASE

Ignore | Ignore All
Change | Change All
Add | Suggest
AutoCorrect
Undo Last | Cancel

Microsoft Excel

The spell check is complete for the entire sheet.

OK

✓ **Adding Words to the Dictionary**
To add new words to the Excel spelling dictionary, choose **Add** in the Spelling dialog box.

⚠ **WARNING**
The spell checker is not infallible. If you typed through when you meant thorough, the spell checker won't catch the error. Proofreading is the final line of defense against error.

1 To spell-check an entire worksheet, press **Ctrl+Home** to make cell **A1** the active cell. To spell-check only a group of cells, select the cells.

2 Click the **Spelling** button on the Standard toolbar. The Spelling dialog box displays the first occurrence of an apparently misspelled word.

3 In the Spelling dialog box, choose **Change** to accept Excel's suggested change, or choose any of the alternative suggestions and click **Change**.

4 Continue clicking **Ignore** or **Change** for each potential error. Click **OK** when Excel announces the end of the spell check.

Task 14: Finding and Replacing Data

Global Replacements and Corrections

Excel's Find feature searches through the worksheet for any data—text or numbers—you are seeking. The Replace feature substitutes the data you designate for the data found by Find.

Start Here

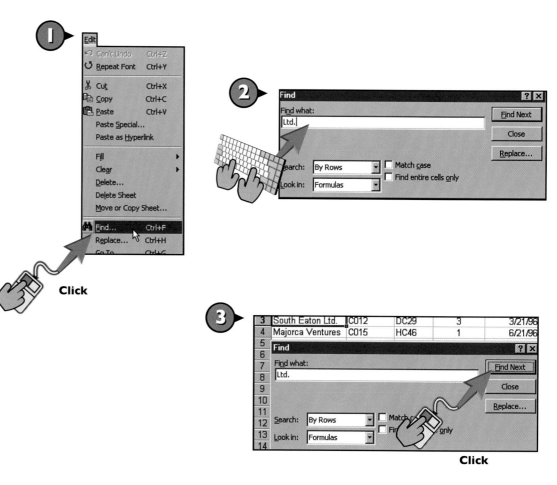

Click

Click

 Moving the Dialog Boxes

If the Find or Replace dialog box obscures your view, point at the dialog box title bar, hold down the left mouse button, and drag the dialog box out of the way.

 Finding More Than Formulas

The default Look In setting in the Find dialog box is Formulas, but Find uncovers what you're looking for, even if it isn't in a formula.

1 Choose **Edit, Find** to summon the Find dialog box.

2 In the Find What edit box, type the data you seek.

3 Click **Find Next** to find the first occurrence of the data. Find selects the cell containing the data.

Next Step

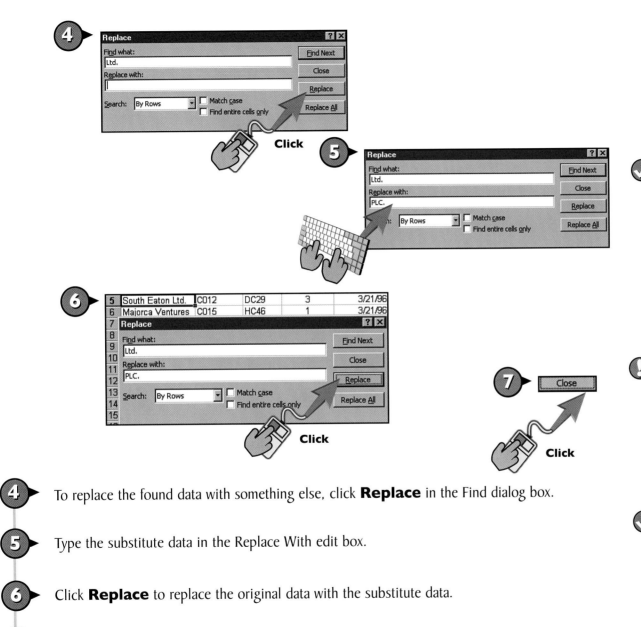

Click

Click

Click

Case Sensitive?
If you're looking for text you know is either upper- or lowercase, click the **Match Case** check box in the Find or Replace dialog box. Then be sure to type the sought-for text with the correct combination of upper- and lowercase characters.

WARNING
The **Replace All** button should be used with care. It replaces every occurrence of the data with your typed replacement, whether you intended the replacement or not.

Finding in a Range
To find and replace in only a section of the worksheet, select the range before you use the **Find** and **Replace** commands.

4 ▶ To replace the found data with something else, click **Replace** in the Find dialog box.

5 ▶ Type the substitute data in the Replace With edit box.

6 ▶ Click **Replace** to replace the original data with the substitute data.

7 ▶ Continue clicking **Find Next** or **Replace** in the Replace dialog box. Click **Close** when you have finished.

End
Task

Task 15: Undoing or Redoing Your Last Edit

Taking Back or Repeating a Change

Some edits would have been better left undone. Undo is an essential feature that can save you from yourself. If you change your mind and decide your original edit was right after all, just click **Redo** to bring it back.

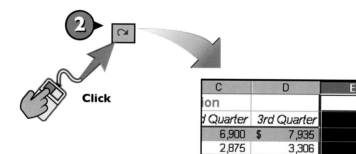

✓ **Undoing Several Actions**

You can undo (reverse) several of your recent worksheet changes. See Task 16 for specific steps on undoing multiple actions.

✓ **Be Certain What Will Be Undone**

The Undo option on the Edit menu displays your last action—handy if you're not sure what you're about to undo or redo.

Click

1 To undo your last action, click the **Undo** button on the Standard toolbar. The worksheet returns to its former state, as though the last action had never occurred.

2 If you change your mind about undoing your edits, click the **Redo** button on the Standard toolbar. Your original edit returns.

Task 16: Undoing and Redoing Multiple Edits

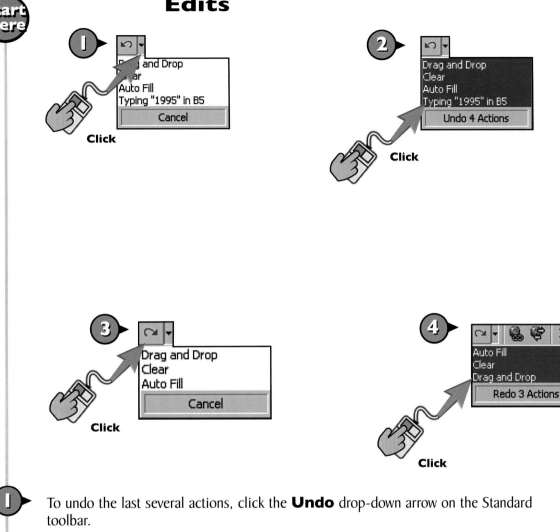

1 Click

2 Click

3 Click

4 Click

Retracing or Repeating Your Steps

When you've made several changes to a worksheet, it's easy to undo them all. It's just as easy to redo them.

1 To undo the last several actions, click the **Undo** drop-down arrow on the Standard toolbar.

2 Point to the action you want to undo. Excel automatically highlights that action and all other actions that happened after it. Click to undo the actions.

3 To redo several actions, click the **Redo** drop-down arrow on the Standard toolbar.

4 Point to the actions you want to redo. Excel automatically highlights that action and all other actions that happened after it. Click to redo them.

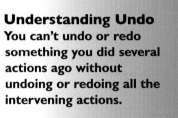

Understanding Undo
You can't undo or redo something you did several actions ago without undoing or redoing all the intervening actions.

Inactive Toolbar Buttons
If there aren't actions you can undo or redo, the **Undo** and **Redo** buttons on the Standard toolbar are grayed out and inoperative.

End Task

Page
51

Task 17: Correcting Spelling with AutoCorrect

AutoCorrect Corrects on the Fly

AutoCorrect fixes typos and misspellings as you make them, automatically.

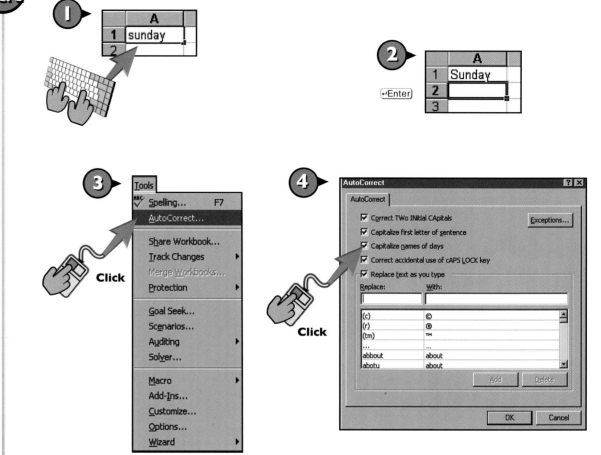

Click

Click

✓ **Deactivate AutoCorrect**
To turn off AutoCorrect, click **Tools, Options, Edit.** Click the **Enable AutoComplete for Cell Values** check box to clear the check mark. Click **OK** to save the change.

✓ **Invoking AutoCorrect**
AutoCorrect changes are made only after you press **Enter** or **Tab** to save the cell value.

1 Type **sunday** in a blank cell.

2 Press **Enter**; Excel automatically corrects "sunday" to "Sunday."

3 To modify any of the types of corrections AutoCorrect makes, click **Tools, AutoCorrect**.

4 In the AutoCorrect dialog box, click any of the check boxes to clear the check marks and stop AutoCorrect from correcting these types of errors.

Task 18: Adding AutoCorrect Entries

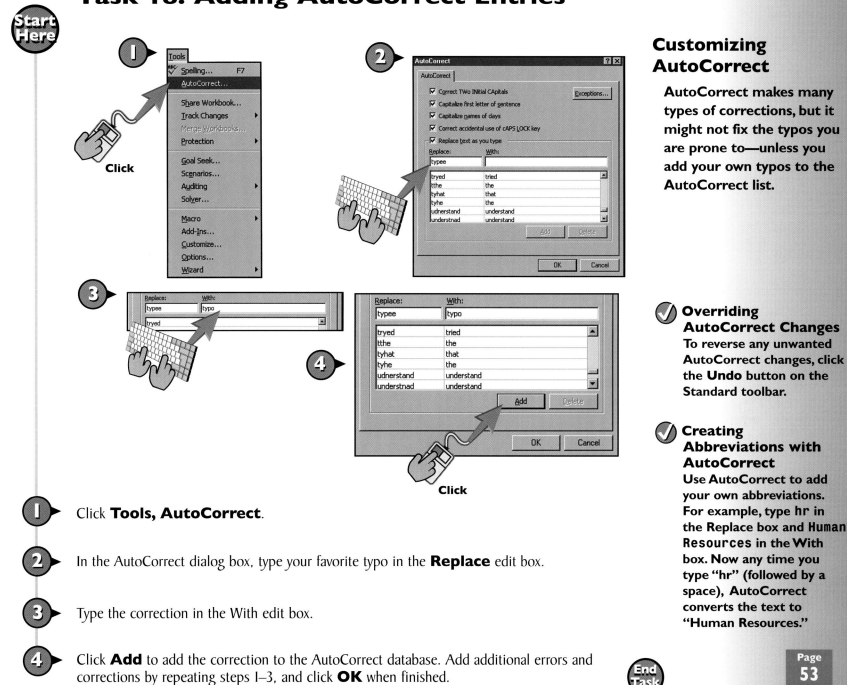

Customizing AutoCorrect

AutoCorrect makes many types of corrections, but it might not fix the typos you are prone to—unless you add your own typos to the AutoCorrect list.

✔ Overriding AutoCorrect Changes
To reverse any unwanted AutoCorrect changes, click the **Undo** button on the Standard toolbar.

✔ Creating Abbreviations with AutoCorrect
Use AutoCorrect to add your own abbreviations. For example, type **hr** in the Replace box and **Human Resources** in the With box. Now any time you type "hr" (followed by a space), AutoCorrect converts the text to "Human Resources."

1 Click **Tools, AutoCorrect**.

2 In the AutoCorrect dialog box, type your favorite typo in the **Replace** edit box.

3 Type the correction in the With edit box.

4 Click **Add** to add the correction to the AutoCorrect database. Add additional errors and corrections by repeating steps 1–3, and click **OK** when finished.

Page
53

Managing Workbooks and Worksheets

Excel files are called workbooks. All your work in Excel is kept in workbooks, and workbooks in turn are kept in folders. The system is a simple one, with the added advantage of being easily customized.

Part 4 looks at Excel's filing system. You'll learn how to track down lost workbooks and how to organize workbooks in ways that make them hard to lose again.

Additionally, you'll learn how to display multiple workbooks on the screen simultaneously, move and copy specific data from one worksheet to another, and move and copy entire worksheets.

Tasks

Task 1: Opening Workbooks

Getting to Your Files

By default, your workbooks are automatically saved in the **My Documents** folder. Everything is stored in one place, making it easy to locate your files.

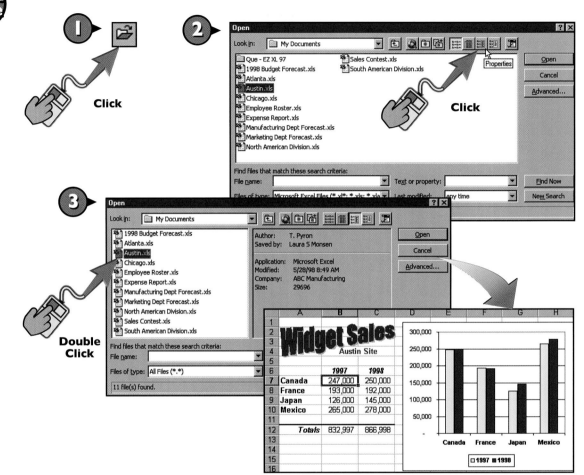

✔ **Adding File Properties**
Open the file you want to work with and choose **File, Properties**. Click the **Summary** tab and fill in the desired properties; then click **OK**.

✔ **Locating Files in Other Folders**
If your files are not stored in My Documents, click the **Look In** drop-down arrow in the Open dialog box and double-click the folder to display any Excel files in the selected folder.

To open a workbook, click the **Open** button on the Standard toolbar.

The Open dialog box appears, displaying the Excel files in the My Documents folder. By default, only the names of the files are listed. Click the **Properties** button.

The screen display changes, showing the names of the files on the left and properties about the selected file on the right. Double-click a file to open it.

Task 2: Finding Workbooks

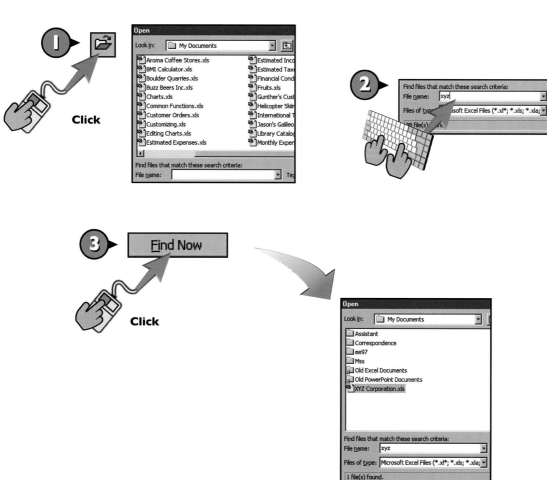

Click

① ② ③ Find Now

Click

Locating Workbooks

Can't remember what you called that workbook or where you put it? Excel has tools to help you find misplaced work. You can search for files by the filename, file type, or date it was last modified and saved.

✅ **Search for Recently Used Files**
If you know approximately when you last worked on a file but you don't remember its name, use the **Last Modified** feature in the Open dialog box to narrow your search. Click the **Last Modified** drop-down arrow, and choose one of the periods on the menu.

① Click the **Open** button on the Standard toolbar to display the Open dialog box.

② If you don't remember the precise workbook name, type part of the name—a single word is enough—in the File Name text box.

③ Choose **Find Now** to see a list of all files whose names contain the word you typed.

✅ **Advanced Search Techniques**
If your workbook can't be turned up with the steps in this task, see Task 3.

Searching Through Subfolders

When subfolders begin to proliferate, files are easily lost. If you remember neither the filename nor the folder where the workbook was stored, but you remember some unique content within the workbook, you can search for the workbook based on that content.

✓ **Searching Your Workbooks for a Phrase**

If you can remember a key phrase from a lost workbook, type the entire phrase, enclosed in quotation marks, in the Text or Property text box of the Open dialog box.

⊘ **WARNING**

An apparent Excel bug caused system crashes on two different computers when I searched folders and subfolders by Text or Property. Make sure to save your work before attempting any similar searches.

Task 3: Searching for Workbooks by Content

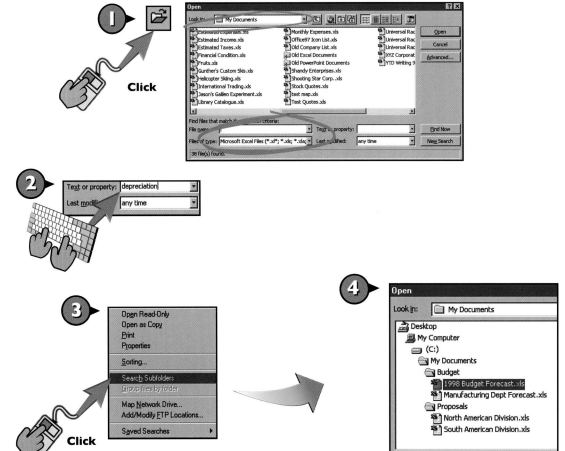

1. Click the **Open** button. In the Open dialog box, check that the default settings are in place: Look In should be set to My Documents; Files of Type should be Microsoft Excel Files.

2. In the **Text or property** text box, type any identifying or unique text you remember from the workbook—this might be cell data, a row or column header, a title, or a label.

3. Click the **Commands and Settings** button on the Open dialog box toolbar and choose **Search Subfolders**.

4. Any workbooks containing the text you typed in step 2 are displayed.

Task 4: Creating a New Folder or Subfolder

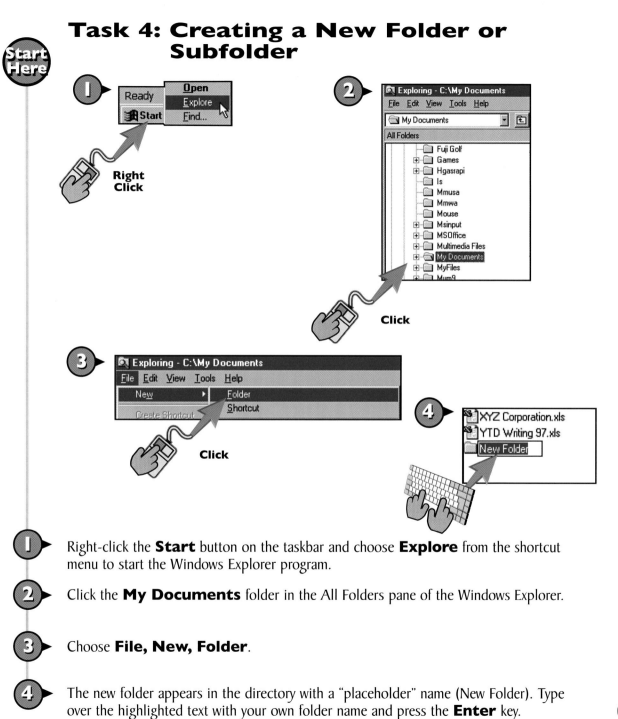

Easy File Management

As workbooks begin to pile up, you can create new folders or subfolders to organize your files. Using folders makes workbooks easier to find, back up, and delete when they're no longer needed.

1. Right-click the **Start** button on the taskbar and choose **Explore** from the shortcut menu to start the Windows Explorer program.

2. Click the **My Documents** folder in the All Folders pane of the Windows Explorer.

3. Choose **File, New, Folder**.

4. The new folder appears in the directory with a "placeholder" name (New Folder). Type over the highlighted text with your own folder name and press the **Enter** key.

Moving Multiple Workbooks

To drag multiple workbooks into your new subfolders, click the first workbook and then Ctrl+click each additional workbook. Point at any of the selected workbooks and drag the highlighted group of items to the new subfolder.

Task 5: Opening and Viewing Multiple Workbooks

Seeing More of Your Work

Copying and pasting data between workbooks, or just comparing data in several workbooks, is convenient and easy to do. To work with more than one workbook at the same time, you need to have all the workbooks open.

Start Here

Click

Ctrl + Click

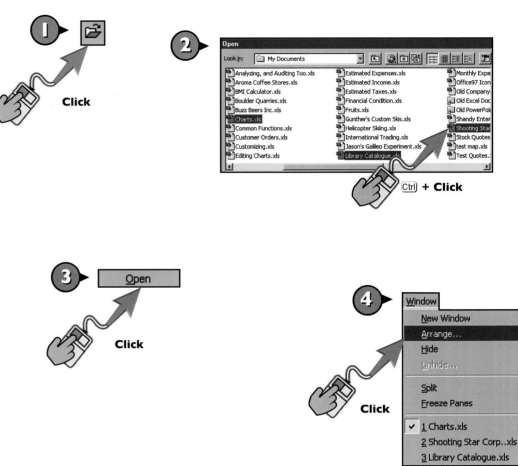

Click

Click

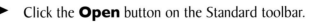

Open

Click

✓ **Maximize a Tiled Window**
To quickly maximize a window, double-click the workbook's title bar. Click the workbook's **Restore** button to shrink it back down again.

✓ **Move a Window**
To move a window around, drag it by the title bar.

① ▶ Click the **Open** button on the Standard toolbar.

② ▶ Click the first workbook you want to open; then Ctrl+Click each additional workbook to be opened.

③ ▶ Click **Open** in the Open dialog box to open all the workbooks at once, in full screen windows.

④ ▶ Choose **Window, Arrange**.

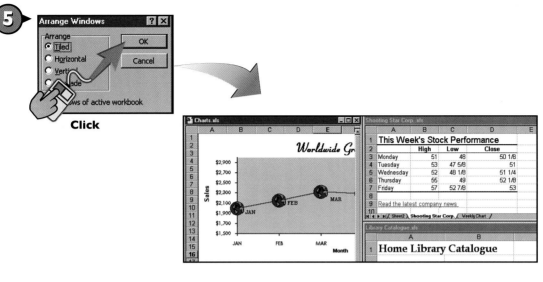

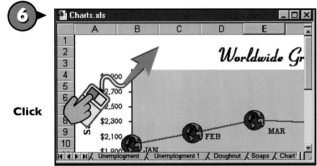

5 ► Choose **Tiled** and click **OK** in the Arrange Windows dialog box. All the open workbooks are displayed in windows, each with its own scrollbars for viewing.

6 ► Click anywhere inside a displayed window to activate it. The active window has a colored title bar and scrollbars.

Task 6: Naming Worksheets

Organizing Worksheets with Names

The default worksheet names—Sheet1, Sheet2, and so on—have the virtue of brevity, but they aren't very descriptive. You can quickly replace them with more meaningful names.

✅ **Duplicates Not Allowed**
You cannot use duplicate worksheet names in the same workbook. Each name must be unique.

✅ **Sheet Name Restrictions**
Each *sheet tab* holds up to 31 characters, including spaces. The following characters are not allowed in sheet tab names:
/ \ * [ ] ? :

✅ **Adding and Deleting Sheets**
To add a worksheet to a workbook, choose **Insert, Worksheet**. To remove a worksheet, choose **Edit, Delete Sheet**.

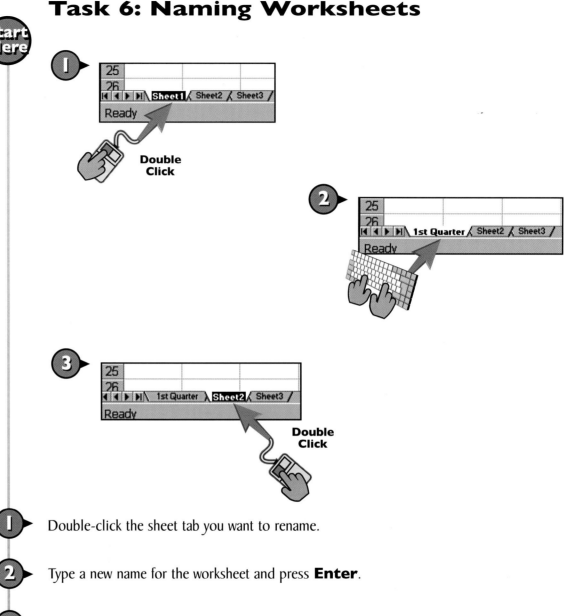

Start Here

Double Click

Double Click

1. Double-click the sheet tab you want to rename.

2. Type a new name for the worksheet and press **Enter**.

3. Double-click the next sheet tab you want to rename.

End Task

Task 7: Copying Worksheets

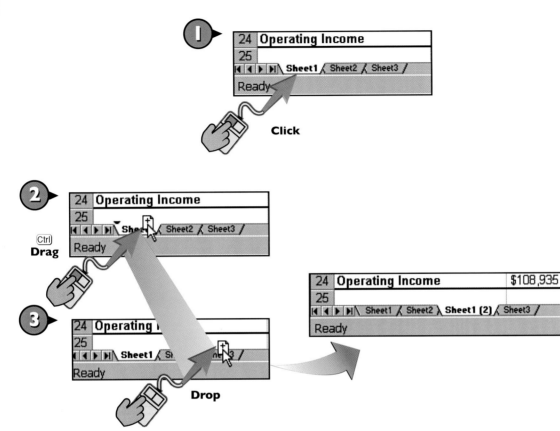

Click

Drag (Ctrl)

Drop

Duplicating Worksheets

Copying a worksheet is handy whenever a new worksheet is going to replicate most or all of the content and formatting of an existing worksheet. To accomplish this, use a technique called drag and drop. See Task 10 to learn how to rearrange the order of the worksheets in a workbook.

✔ **Don't Like to Drag?**
See Task 9 for steps on copying or moving worksheets to other workbooks.

✔ **Renaming Worksheets**
Copied worksheets take the name of the original worksheet tab and add a number in parenthesis, as in "Sheet1." See Task 6 for steps to rename worksheets.

1 ▶ Click the sheet tab of the worksheet you want to copy.

2 ▶ Point at the selected sheet tab, hold down the **Ctrl** key, and hold down the **left mouse button**. The mouse pointer now shows a page symbol with a plus sign.

3 ▶ Drag the worksheet tab to the location where you want the copy to be placed. A small black triangle indicates where the copy will go. Release the **mouse button** to drop the copy into place; then release the **Ctrl** key.

Copying and Cutting Data Between Worksheets

When you don't want to copy an entire worksheet but need some of the data from a worksheet, select the data and then copy and paste (or cut and paste) it into another worksheet.

Task 8: Sharing Data Between Worksheets

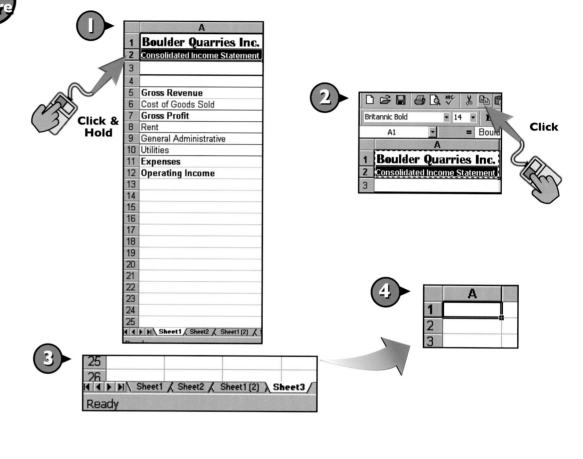

✓ **Copy to Multiple Sheets**

To copy data to multiple worksheets, click each additional worksheet tab and destination cell, and click the **Paste** button on the Standard toolbar.

1 ▶ Select the cells you want to copy into another worksheet.

2 ▶ Click the **Copy** button on the Standard toolbar.

3 ▶ Click the sheet tab of the worksheet where you want the data to go.

4 ▶ Click the cell in the destination worksheet in the upper-left corner of the range into which you want to copy the selected cells.

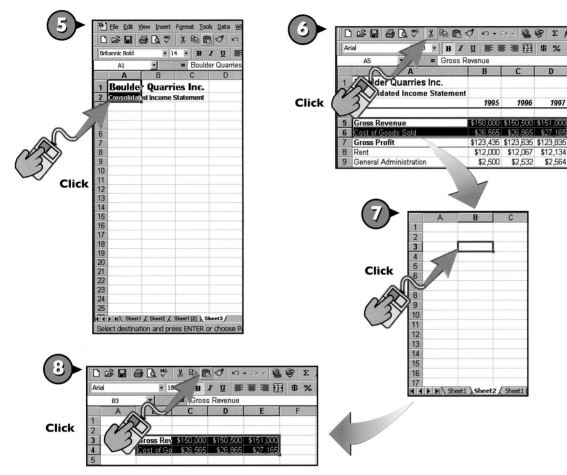

5 Click the **Paste** button on the Standard toolbar to paste a copy of the data in the new location.

6 To move data between worksheets instead of copying it, select the data to be moved and click the **Cut** button on the Standard toolbar.

7 Click the sheet tab and cell of the worksheet where you want the data to be moved.

8 Click the **Paste** button on the Standard toolbar to move the data into its new location. See Part 2, Task 7, to learn how to adjust the column width.

⚠ WARNING
If you paste data into cells with existing content, you overwrite that content. Press **Ctrl+Z** immediately to undo any damage, and try using **Insert, Copied Cells** instead.

Placing Worksheets in the Right Workbooks

As you build more extensive workbooks, you might decide you need to move or copy a worksheet from one workbook (the source) to another workbook (the target).

 Open All Necessary Files

Before you can move or copy worksheets between workbooks, the files must be open in Excel. See Task 1 for steps on opening files.

 Moving or Copying Multiple Worksheets

To select more than one worksheet to move or copy, click the first sheet tab, press the **Ctrl** key, and click each additional sheet tab.

Task 9: Moving or Copying Worksheets Between Workbooks

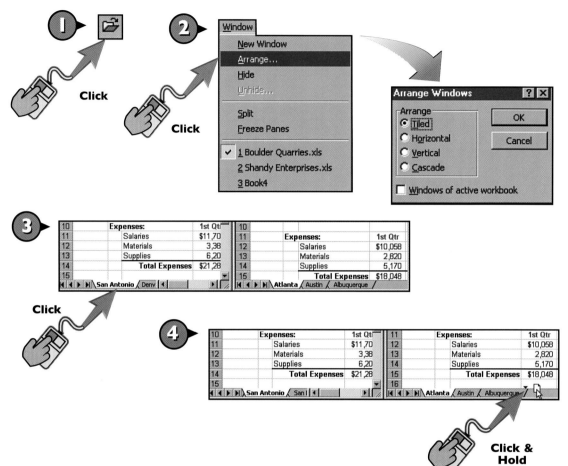

1 Open the source and target workbooks. See Task 1 if you've forgotten how to open files.

2 Choose **Window, Arrange**, and then choose **Tiled** to arrange the workbooks on the screen. See Task 5 if you need a refresher on this process.

3 Click the sheet tab of the worksheet you want to move or copy.

4 To move a worksheet, hold down the left mouse button and drag the worksheet into position. To copy a worksheet, hold down the **Ctrl** key as you drag.

Task 10: Moving Worksheets Within the Workbook

Start Here

1

	A	B	C	D	E	F	G	H	I
1				ABC Consulting Corporation					
2				San Antonio Division					
3									
4		Revenues:		1st Qtr	2nd Qtr	3rd Qtr	4th Qtr	Annual	
5			Consulting	$14,000	$15,000	$15,645	$12,050	$56,695	
6			Bids and Proposals	7,200	6,575	8,000	5,000	26,775	
7			Misc	7,000	4,500	6,500	7,200	25,200	
8			Total Revenues	$28,200	$26,075	$30,145	$24,250	$108,670	
9									
10		Expenses:		1st Qtr	2nd Qtr	3rd Qtr	4th Qtr	Annual	
11			Salaries	$11,700	$11,160	$12,902	$10,379	$46,141	
12			Materials	3,384	3,129	3,617	2,910	13,040	
13			Operating Costs	6,204	5,737	6,632	5,335	23,907	
14			Total Expenses	$21,288	20,026	$23,151	$18,624	$83,089	
15									
16		Net Revenues		$6,912	$6,049		$5,626	$25,581	
17									

San Antonio / Denver / San Francisco /

Ready

Click

2

13		Operating Costs	6,204	5,737	6,632
14		Total Expenses	$21,288	$20,026	$23,151
15					
16		Net Revenues	$6,912	$6,049	$6,994
17					

San Antonio / Denver / San Francisco /

Ready

Drag

3

13		Operating Costs	6,204	5,737	6
14		Total Expenses	$21,288	$20,026	
15					
16		Net Revenues	$6,912	$6	
17					

San Antonio / Denver / San Francisco /

Ready

Drop

13		Operating Costs	6,204	5,737	6,632
14		Total Expenses	$21,288	$20,026	$23,151
15					
16		Net Revenues	$6,912	$6,049	$6,994
17					

Denver / San Francisco \ San Antonio /

Ready

Rearranging the Order of the Worksheets

Moving a worksheet within a workbook is a simple "drag and drop" movement with the mouse. See Task 7 to learn how to copy worksheets.

1 Click the sheet tab of the worksheet you want to move.

2 Point at the selected sheet tab and hold down the left mouse button. The mouse pointer displays a page symbol.

3 Drag the worksheet tab to the location where you want the worksheet to be placed; a small black triangle indicates where the worksheet will go. Release the mouse button to drop the worksheet into place.

✓ Drag and Drop to Other Workbooks
See Task 9 to move or copy worksheets to other workbooks.

End Task

Task 11: Freezing Panes for Convenient Scrolling

Keeping Headers in View While Scrolling

When worksheets get long, scrolling to the bottom or right of the worksheet puts headers out of sight. You can freeze the titles at the top or left so they remain in view as you scroll.

Start Here

1

	A	B	C	D	E
1	ABC Manufacturing Corporation				
2	National Sales Analysis				
3					
4	State	% Sales	January	February	March
5	*Western Sector*				
6	Arizona	5.94%	655,900	682,792	674,598
7	California	2.47%	132,900	125,723	141,816
8	Colorado	6.77%	865,330	888,694	639,860
9	Montana	6.77%	865,330	888,694	639,860
10	Nebraska	2.47%	132,900	125,723	141,816
11	Nevada	7.88%	989,560	712,483	703,933
12	New Mexico	3.28%	230,970	196,325	221,454
13	Oklahoma	5.31%	754,980	745,920	776,503
14	Texas	1.33%	145,300	163,898	168,324
15	Utah	2.47%	132,900	125,723	141,816
16	Wyoming	5.31%	754,980	745,920	776,503

NATIONAL

Click

2

Window

New Window
Arrange...
Hide
Unhide...

Split
Freeze Panes

✓ 1 National.xls
2 WL Training Company...s

Click

3

	A	B	C	D	E
1	ABC Manufacturing Corporation				
2	National Sales Analysis				
3					
4	State	% Sales	January	February	March
12	New Mexico	3.28%	230,970	196,325	22
13	Oklahoma	5.31%	754,980	745,920	7
14	Texas	1.33%	145,300	163,898	16
15	Utah	2.47%	132,900	125,723	141,816
16	Wyoming	5.31%	754,980	745,920	776,503
17					
18	*Southern Sector*				
19	Alabama	7.88%	989,560	712,483	703,933
20	Arkansas	2.47%	132,900	125,723	141,816
21	Florida	1.33%	145,300	163,898	168,324
22	Georgia	5.94%	655,900	682,792	674,598
23	Kentucky	6.77%	865,330	888,694	639,860

NATIONAL

4

Window

New Window
Arrange...
Hide
Unhide...

Split
Unfreeze Panes

✓ 1 National.xls
2 WL Training Company.X

Click

✓ Selecting the Correct Cell

When you freeze panes in Excel, you freeze titles above and to the left of the active cell. To freeze the titles in rows 1–4, for example, make cell A5 the active cell. To freeze titles in column A, make cell B1 the active cell. To freeze both rows 1–4 and column A, make cell B5 your active cell.

✓ Changing Which Titles are Frozen

If you already have titles frozen in a worksheet, you must unfreeze the panes before you can freeze other titles.

1 To freeze the titles at the top of the worksheet, select a cell in column A in the row directly below the titles.

2 Choose **Window, Freeze Panes**.

3 A dark line appears, indicating where the titles are frozen. Drag the scroll box down to see additional rows; the titles remain onscreen.

4 To unfreeze the titles, choose **Window, Unfreeze Panes**.

Next Step

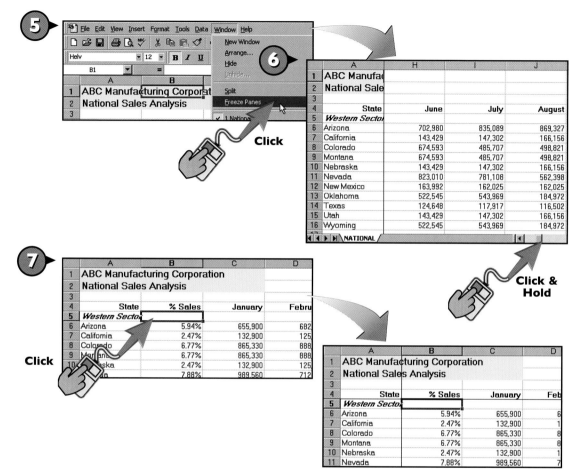

Click

Click & Hold

5 ▶ To freeze the titles in the columns on the left side of the worksheet, select a cell in row 1 immediately to the right of the titles.

6 ▶ A dark line appears, indicating where the titles are frozen. Drag the scroll box to the right to see additional columns; the titles remain onscreen.

7 ▶ To freeze titles in both columns and rows, select a cell below and to the right of the intersection of the titles and choose **Window, Freeze Panes**. Dark lines appear, indicating where the titles are frozen.

 Freezing Panes is Permanent
If you save the workbook with the frozen titles, the titles will still be frozen the next time you open the workbook (until you unfreeze them).

Splitting Windows
An alternative to freezing worksheet titles is to split the worksheet window. You can then scroll each split section independently. To split a worksheet window, position the active cell where you want the split and choose **Window, Split**.

Formatting Worksheets

Formatting has everything to do with the appearance of the worksheet. A well-formatted worksheet is more than a pretty face, because rows and columns of numbers are not inherently engaging. To avoid inducing somnolence on the reader's part, your own included, your work deserves all the dressing-up you can give it.

Less is more when it comes to formatting worksheets. A few small touches can make the difference between a gray expanse of cells and a readable piece of work. Part 5 looks at the host of formatting features you can apply to your worksheets.

Tasks

Task I: Formatting Currency

Dollars—Also ¥, F, and £

Formatting cells with dollar signs is a one-click operation. To get yen, pounds sterling, and francs, requires a little more effort, but not much more.

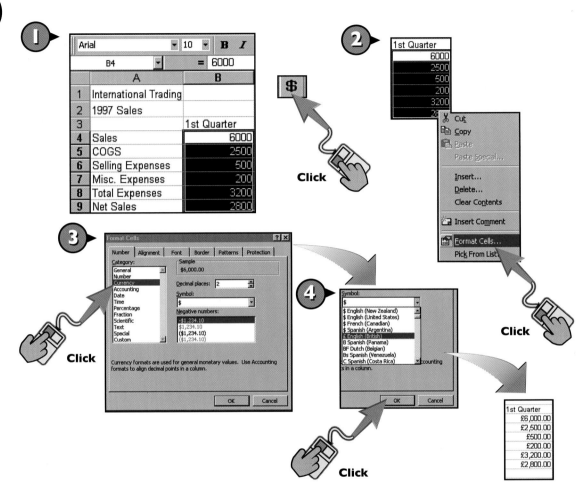

✓ Changing the Number of Decimals Displayed

To increase or decrease the number of decimal places Excel displays, see Task 4.

✓ Removing Cell Formats

To clear all the formatting in a cell but retain cell contents, select the cell and choose **Edit, Clear, Formats**.

① For U.S. dollars, select the cell or range containing numbers you want to format. Then click the **Currency Style** button on the Formatting toolbar.

② For pounds sterling, French francs, and other currencies, select the cells. Then right-click in any selected cell and choose **Format Cells** from the shortcut menu.

③ On the Number tab in the Format Cells dialog box, click the **Currency** category.

④ In the Symbol drop-down list, choose a currency and click **OK**. The Format Cells dialog box disappears and the currency format is applied to the cells.

Task 2: Formatting Dates

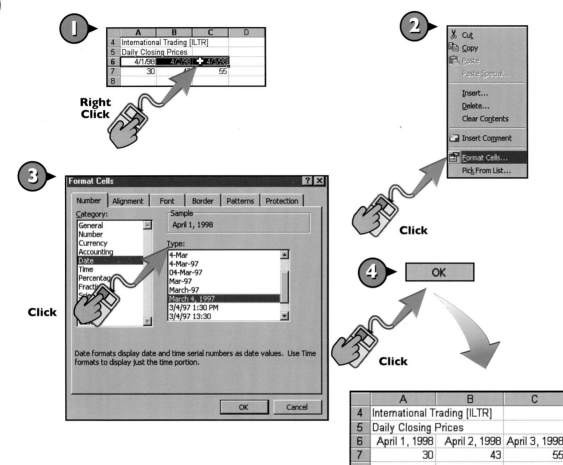

The Shape of Dates to Come

Part 2, Task 9, contained information about entering numbers as dates. When you type a date in a standard format, such as Day/Month/Year or Day-Month-Year, Excel recognizes the number as a date. After you enter the date, you can choose from many other formats.

1 Select the cell or range containing dates whose formats you want to change. Then right-click in any of the selected cells to display the shortcut menu.

2 Choose **Format Cells** from the shortcut menu.

3 On the Number tab of the Format Cells dialog box, choose the **Date** category and select a format from the Type list.

4 Click **OK**; the Format Cells dialog box disappears and the date format is applied to the cells.

 Formatting Time
Times entered in the formats described in Part 2, Task 9, can be formatted in various styles, using the method for dates outlined in this task.

Keyboard Shortcut
A quick way to display the Format Cells dialog box is to press **Ctrl+1**.

 End Task

Task 3: Formatting Negative Numbers

Displaying Numbers in the Red, in Red

Formatting is good for emphasizing aspects of the worksheet. Negative number formats vary from red and emphatic to discreet parentheses, depending on your needs.

Start Here

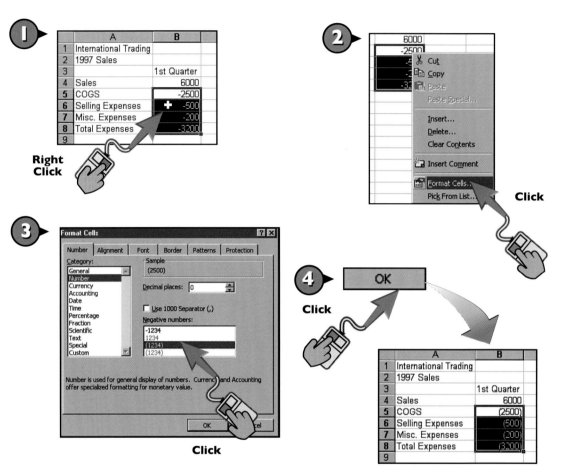

Right Click

Click

Click

Click

Click

✓ **Entering Negative Numbers**
To type a negative number, precede the number with the dash [–] symbol, such as –200.

✓ **Black and White Printer?**
If you're planning to print the worksheet and you have a black and white printer, skip the red format for negative numbers.

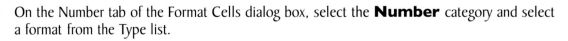

I Select the cell or range containing the negative numbers whose formats you want to change. Then right-click any of the selected cells to display the shortcut menu.

2 Choose **Format Cells** on the shortcut menu.

3 On the Number tab of the Format Cells dialog box, select the **Number** category and select a format from the Type list.

4 Click **OK**; the Format Cells dialog box disappears and the negative number format is applied to the cells.

End Task

Task 4: Increasing and Decreasing Decimal Places

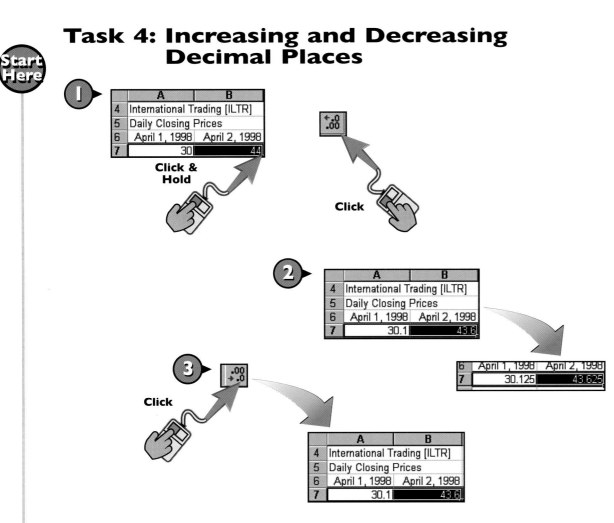

Click & Hold

Click

Click

Numbers with More or Less Precision

For scientists who require numbers displayed to the tenth decimal place, or number crunchers interested in rounding up for simplicity's sake, increasing or decreasing decimal places is an easy chore.

① Select the cell or range whose numbers you want to format.

② Click the **Increase Decimal** button on the Formatting toolbar to add one decimal place. Click repeatedly for additional decimal places.

③ Click the **Decrease Decimal** button on the Formatting toolbar to remove one decimal place. Click repeatedly for fewer decimal places.

When Formatting Results in ######
If the result of formatting a number displays ###### in the cell, the number (with the format) is too long for the width of the column. Widen the column or use the **Decrease Decimal** button to shorten the number.

Task 5: Formatting Fractions

Mixed Numbers

Type 1/4 in a cell, and Excel displays 4-Jan. Typing 2/67 results in Feb-67. Entering a fraction shouldn't be a challenge, and it's not—provided you know how to tell Excel you want a fraction, not a date.

Start Here

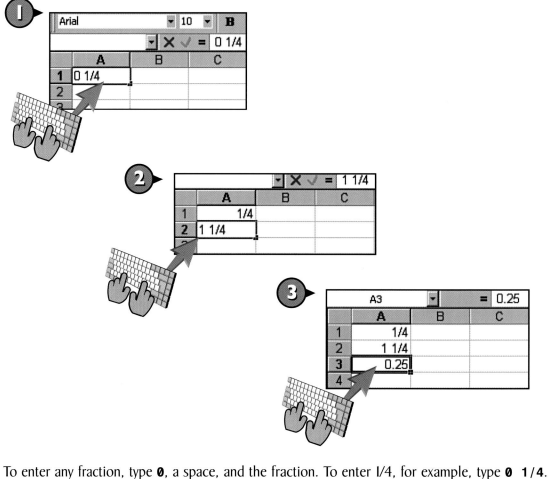

✓ How Excel Stores Fractions

If you type 0 1/4, Excel displays 1/4 in the cell but stores the number as 0.25 internally (which displays in the Formula bar).

✓ Formatting Alternative

Instead of typing in the leading zero (0 1/4) for a fraction, format the cells before you type the numbers. On the Number tab of the Format Cells dialog box, select the **Fraction** category and choose the format **Up to Two Digits**.

1. To enter any fraction, type **0**, a space, and the fraction. To enter 1/4, for example, type **0 1/4**.

2. To enter mixed numbers, type the whole number, a space, and the fraction. To enter 1 1/4, for example, type **1 1/4**.

3. Decimal fractions automatically display as decimals. Type **0.25**, for example, and Excel displays 0.25.

End Task

Task 6: Applying Boldface, Italic, or Underline

Start Here

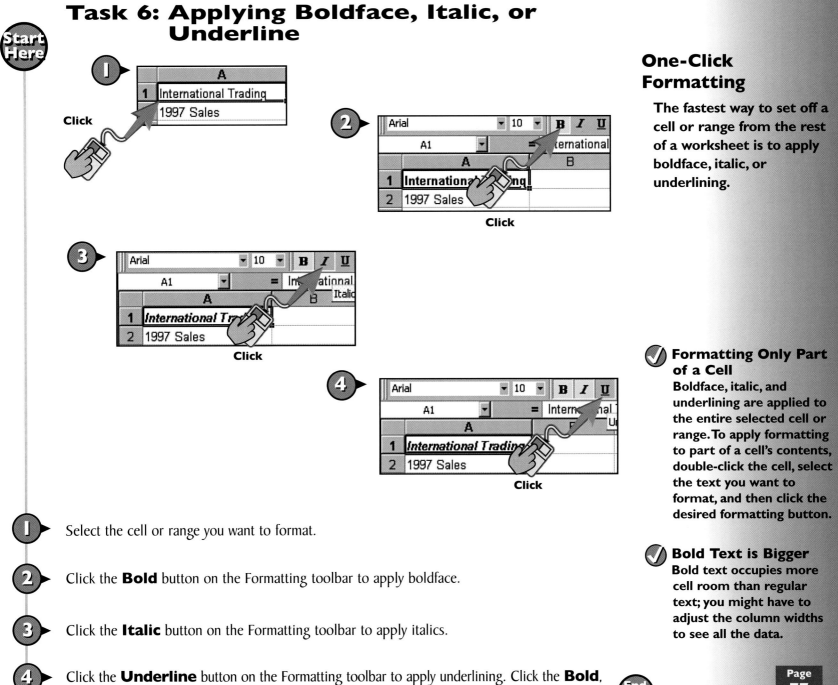

One-Click Formatting

The fastest way to set off a cell or range from the rest of a worksheet is to apply boldface, italic, or underlining.

✓ **Formatting Only Part of a Cell**
Boldface, italic, and underlining are applied to the entire selected cell or range. To apply formatting to part of a cell's contents, double-click the cell, select the text you want to format, and then click the desired formatting button.

✓ **Bold Text is Bigger**
Bold text occupies more cell room than regular text; you might have to adjust the column widths to see all the data.

1 Select the cell or range you want to format.

2 Click the **Bold** button on the Formatting toolbar to apply boldface.

3 Click the **Italic** button on the Formatting toolbar to apply italics.

4 Click the **Underline** button on the Formatting toolbar to apply underlining. Click the **Bold**, **Italic**, or **Underline** buttons again to remove any of the formats from the selected cells.

End Task

Data Alignment

By default, Excel aligns numbers on the right of the cell and text on the left. One click centers any kind of data in the cell or aligns it right or left.

Task 7: Indenting, Centering, and Aligning Data Left or Right

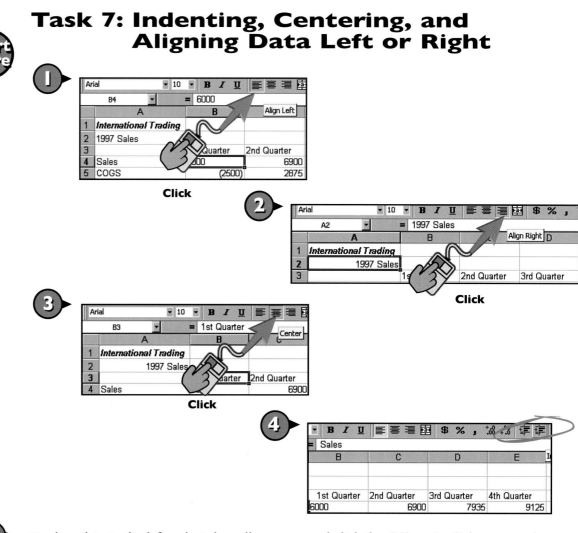

Start Here

Click

Click

Click

✓ **Buttons Turn Alignment On and Off**
The Alignment buttons on the Formatting toolbar are toggles. To remove the alignment you've applied to a selected cell, click the Alignment button again.

✓ **Centering Text Across Columns**
To center text over columns, see Task 10.

1 To align data to the left, select the cell or range and click the **Align Left** button on the Formatting toolbar.

2 To align data to the right, select the cell or range and click the **Align Right** button on the Formatting toolbar.

3 To center data in the cell, select the cell or range and click the **Center** button on the Formatting toolbar.

4 To align data in the cell left or right by one tab stop, click the **Increase Indent** or **Decrease Indent** button on the Formatting toolbar.

End Task

Task 8: Changing Fill Color

Start Here

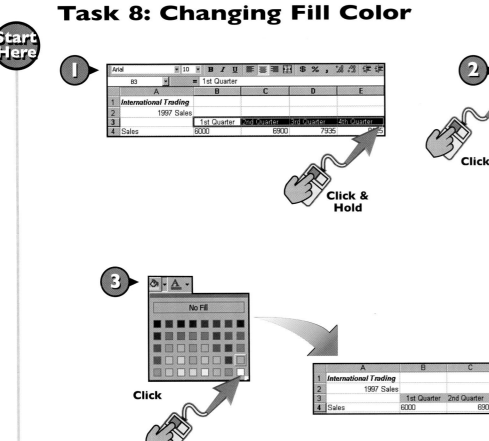

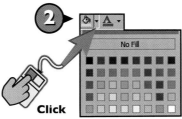

Splashing Color on the Worksheet

Fill is the background color in the cell. The fill is white by default, but you can make it any color you choose. Use a fill color on the title or on the column and row headings to enhance the worksheet appearance.

✅ **Using the Same Color Again**
The last fill color you applied to a cell is displayed on the Fill Color button. To use the same color on other cells, select the cells and click the **Fill Color** button (not the drop-down arrow).

⚠️ **WARNING**
Use light background fill colors with dark text, and dark background fill colors with light text. To change text colors, see Task 13.

1. Select the cell or range you want to color.

2. Click the **Fill Color** drop-down arrow on the Formatting toolbar.

3. Click any color on the palette to apply the color to the selected cell or range.

Task 9: Applying Borders

Borders Make Cells Stand Out

Borders are lines that go around, below, to either side, or above cells or ranges. Borders can also be applied within a range in a grid pattern. Border lines can be thick or thin, double or single.

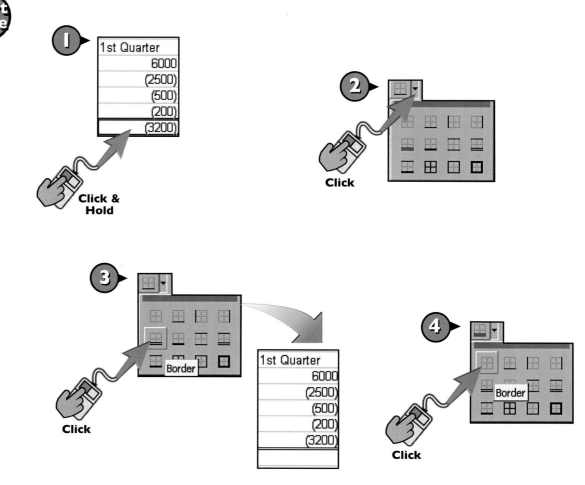

Start Here

Click & Hold

Click

Click

Border

1st Quarter
6000
(2500)
(500)
(200)
(3200)

Border

Click

Changing the Border Color

The default color used with borders is black. To apply another color, see Task 14.

 Select the cell or range to which the border is to be applied.

 Click the **Borders** drop-down arrow on the Formatting toolbar.

Click the border you want to apply to the selected cell or range. The double bottom border is selected in this example.

 Click the first border option in the upper-left corner of the border palette to remove all borders from selected cells or ranges.

 End Task

Task 10: Centering Text over Columns

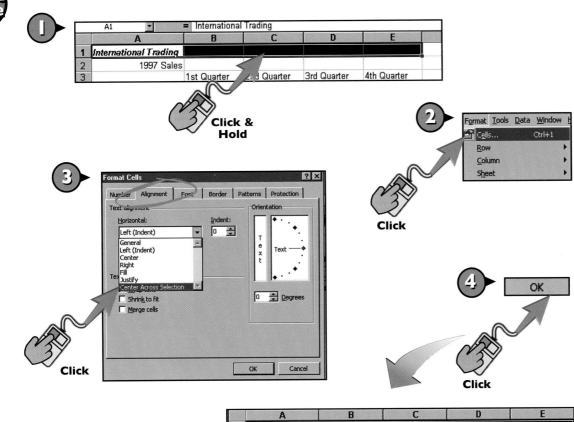

Click & Hold

Click

Click

Click

Centering Titles over Worksheet Data

Centering a title within the cell is accomplished with a click of the Center button on the Formatting toolbar (see Task 7). To Center text across several columns over a table, you need to access the Format Cells dialog box.

① Click the cell containing the title you want to center. Hold down the left mouse button and drag through the row to the right-most column in which the text is to be centered.

② Choose **Format, Cells** to display the Format Cells dialog box.

③ On the Alignment tab of the Format Cells dialog box, click the **Horizontal** drop-down arrow and choose **Center Across Selection.**

④ Click **OK**. The title is centered in the selected cells.

⚠ WARNING
Using the Merge and Center button on the Formatting toolbar can cause problems. If you attempt to center more than one row of headings at a time, data will be lost, and if you need to insert a column in the middle of your worksheet list, you have to unmerge your headings before you can insert the column.

Quick Worksheet Makeovers

Fonts are those named type styles in which all your typing in Excel appears. The default is Arial, a readable and serviceable font, but there are many other choices. Because fonts have a profound effect on the look of your worksheet, the choices are worth exploring.

 Previewing a Font

To see what a font looks like before you apply it to your text, choose **Format, Cells.** In the Format Cells dialog box, click the Font tab. Select a font type and use the Preview section to see how the font will appear.

Task 11: Changing Fonts

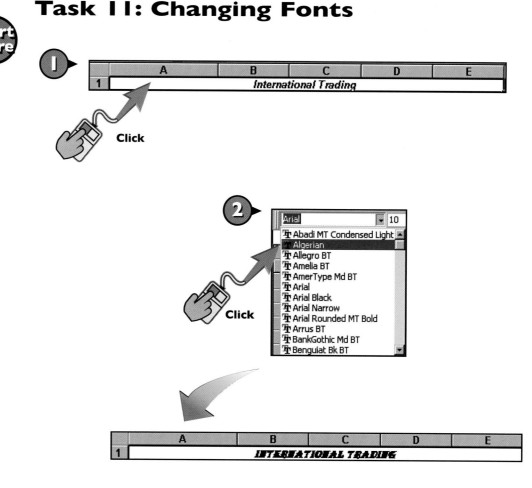

Click

Click

 Select the cell or range whose font you want to change.

 Click the **Font** drop-down arrow on the Formatting toolbar and select a different font. The drop-down list disappears, and the new font is applied to your text.

Task 12: Changing Font Size

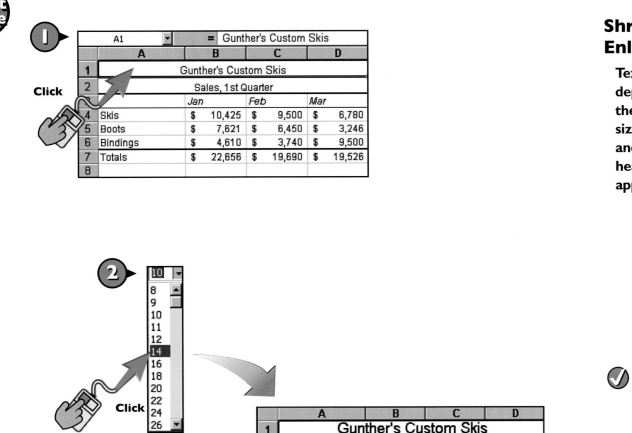

Click

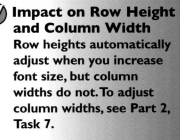

Click

Shrinking or Enlarging Characters

Text can shriek or whisper, depending on the size of the font. Increase the font size of your worksheet titles and column or row headings to enhance their appearance.

1 Select the cell or range whose font size you want to change.

2 Click the **Font Size** drop-down arrow on the Formatting toolbar and choose a font size from the drop-down menu. The menu disappears and the font size is applied to the selected text.

Impact on Row Height and Column Width

Row heights automatically adjust when you increase font size, but column widths do not. To adjust column widths, see Part 2, Task 7.

Understanding Font Sizes

Font sizes are measured in points. An inch contains 72 points, so a 12 point font is 1/6 of an inch high.

Task 13: Changing Font Color

Characters with Color

Black text on a white background is a safe—and readable—choice. But with the widespread use of color printers and with many documents distributed electronically anyway, worksheet color can provide welcome visual variety. Use dark text with a light background fill color, and light text with a dark background fill color. To change background fill colors, see Task 8.

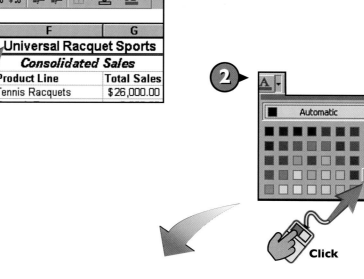

Start Here

Click

Click

Font Color (Gray-25%)

	F	G
Universal Racquet Sports		
Consolidated Sales		
Product Line	**Total Sales**	
Tennis Racquets	$26,000.00	
Squash Racquets	9,000.00	
Badminton Racquets	5,000.00	

✓ Using the Same Color Again

The last font color you applied to a cell is displayed on the Font Color button. To use the same color on other cells, select the cells and click the **Font Color** button (not the drop-down arrow).

1 ▶ Select the cell or range whose font color you want to change.

2 ▶ Click the **Font Color** drop-down arrow on the Formatting toolbar and choose a new color on the menu. The menu disappears and the font color is applied to the selection.

End Task

Task 14: Applying Colored Borders

Start Here

1 Universal Racquet Sports
Consolidated Sales

2 Format
　Cells...　　　　　Ctrl+1
　Row　　　　　　▶
　Column　　　　▶
　Sheet　　　　　▶
　AutoFormat...
　Conditional Formatting...
　Style...

Click

3 Format Cells
Number | Alignment | Font | Border | Patterns | Protection
Presets
None | Outline | Inside
Border
Text
The selected border style can be applied by clicking diagram or the buttons above.
Line Style: None
Color: Automatic
Automatic
Plum

Click

4 Format Cells
Number | Alignment | Font | Border | Patterns | Protection
Presets
None | Outline | Inside
Border
Text
The selected border style can be applied by clicking the presets, preview diagram or the buttons above.
Line Style: None
Color:
OK | Cancel

Universal Racquet Sports
Consolidated Sales

Click

Lines with Color

Colored borders are a subtle and effective way of introducing color into the worksheet without overshadowing the worksheet data.

1 Select a cell or range to which you want to apply the colored border.

2 Choose **Format, Cells**.

3 On the Border tab of the Format Cells dialog box, click the **Color** drop-down arrow and select a color on the menu.

4 Click one or more of the **Border** buttons and choose a **Line Style** if desired. Click **OK** in the Format Cells dialog box to apply the border.

✓ **Changing Border Colors**
To color an existing border, choose a color in the Format Cells dialog box.

End Task

Task 15: Erasing Formatting

Removing Formatting and Leaving Cell Content

You can clear all the formatting applied to a cell, leaving the cell and its contents intact.

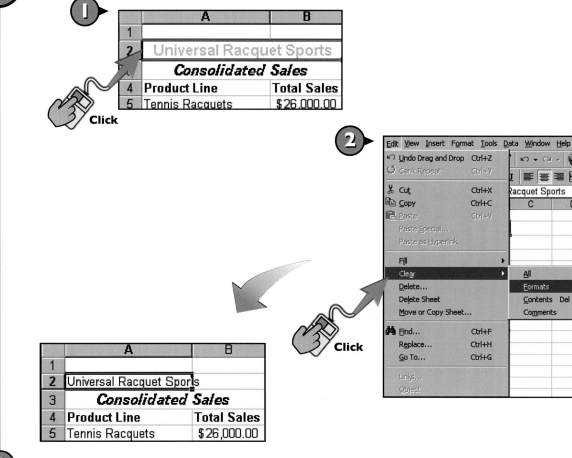

Click

Click

Select the cell or range whose formatting you want to clear.

Click **Edit, Clear, Formats**. All formatting in the selected cells is removed.

 Deleting Cell Data and Formats

To remove both formatting and cell contents, choose **Edit, Clear, All**.

 WARNING

The Edit, Clear, Formats command removes all formatting indiscriminately. To remove only certain formatting, use the Format Cells dialog box to clear the formats one by one.

Task 16: Copying Formats

1

	A	B	C	D	E
1	International Trading Corporation				
2	1997 Sales				
3		1st Quarter	2nd Quarter	3rd Quarter	4th Quarter
4	Sales	$ 6,000.00	$ 6,900.00	$ 7,935.00	$ 9,125.25
5	COGS	2,500	2,875	3,306	3,802
6	Selling Expenses	500	575	661	760
7	Misc. Expenses	200	230	265	304
8	Total Expenses	3200	3680	4232	4866.8
9	Net Sales	$ 2,800.00	$ 3,220.00	$ 3,703.00	$ 4,258.45

Click

2

Click

3

	A	B	C	D	E
3		1st Quarter	2nd Quarter	3rd Quarter	4th Quarter
4	Sales	$ 6,000.00	$ 6,900.00	$ 7,935.00	$ 9,125.25
5	COGS	2,500	2,875	3,306	3,802
6	Selling Expenses	500	575	661	760
7	Misc. Expenses	200	230	265	304
8	Total Expenses	3200	3680	4232	4866.8
9	Net Sales	$ 2,800.00	$ 3,220.00	$ 3,703.00	$ 4,258.45

Click & Hold

	A	B	C	D	E
3		1st Quarter	2nd Quarter	3rd Quarter	4th Quarter
4	Sales	$ 6,000.00	$ 6,900.00	$ 7,935.00	$ 9,125.25
5	COGS	2,500	2,875	3,306	3,802
6	Selling Expenses	500	575	661	760
7	Misc. Expenses	200	230	265	304
8	Total Expenses	$ 3,200.00	$ 3,680.00	$ 4,232.00	$ 4,866.80
9	Net Sales	$ 2,800.00	$ 3,220.00	$ 3,703.00	$ 4,258.45

1 ▶ Select the cell or range that contains the formatting you want to copy.

2 ▶ Click the **Format Painter** button on the Standard toolbar.

3 ▶ The mouse pointer has a paintbrush symbol attached. Click the cell or drag through the range where you want the formatting applied. The new formats are displayed immediately in the cells.

Duplicate Formatting

Getting formatting just right can take a little time. Applying a successful format to other cells on the worksheet takes no time at all. The Format Painter applies a selected format like a painter spreading a coat of paint.

✔ Copying Formats to Multiple Cells
To copy formatting to multiple cells or ranges, double-click the **Format Painter** button. Then click the cells or drag through the ranges where you want the selected format applied. Press **Esc** to stop copying the format.

Task 17: Applying Patterns

Filling Patterns for Emphasis

Patterns, like fill colors, change the background of cells, providing contrast and emphasis in the worksheet.

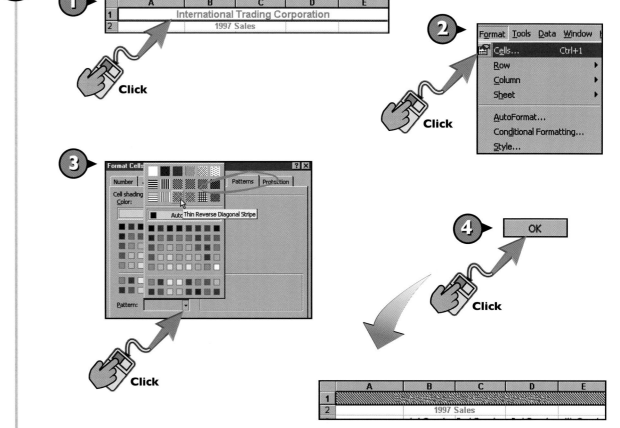

 Select the cell or range where you want to apply a pattern.

2 Choose **Format, Cells** to display the Format Cells dialog box.

3 On the Pattern tab, click the **Pattern** drop-down arrow and choose a pattern from the menu. If desired, choose a pattern color as well.

4 Click **OK** in the Format Cells dialog box to apply the pattern.

Task 18: Applying AutoFormats

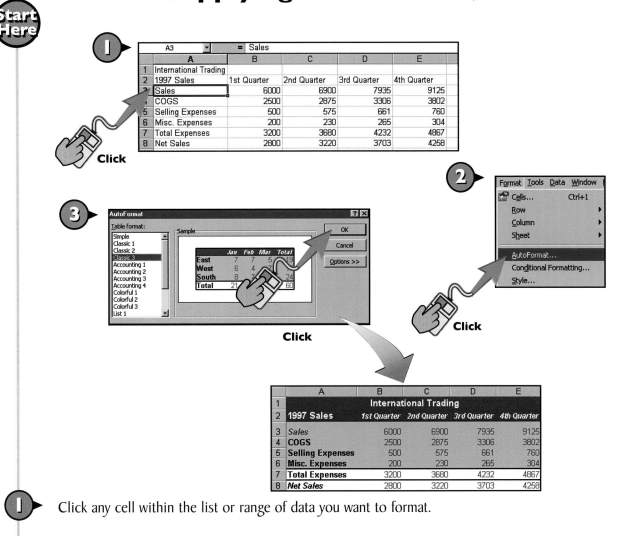

Instant Formatting

Excel includes a selection of prefabricated worksheet formats that save you the trouble of designing formatting yourself. The AutoFormats are easily applied, and just as easily removed if you don't like them.

1. ▶ Click any cell within the list or range of data you want to format.

2. ▶ Click **Format, AutoFormat** to display the AutoFormat dialog box. Excel automatically selects all the cells in the list.

3. ▶ Click a format and use the Sample area to preview the formats. When you find the one you like, click **OK**. The format is applied.

✔️ Applying a Different AutoFormat
To change an applied AutoFormat, click any cell in the list of data and choose **Format, AutoFormat**. Double-click another format. The existing AutoFormat is overwritten with the new choice.

❗ WARNING
Applying an AutoFormat overwrites existing formatting.

Task 19: Modifying AutoFormats

Customizing Canned Formatting

AutoFormats are fast and effective, but sometimes don't provide exactly what you need. You can select which formats the AutoFormat applies.

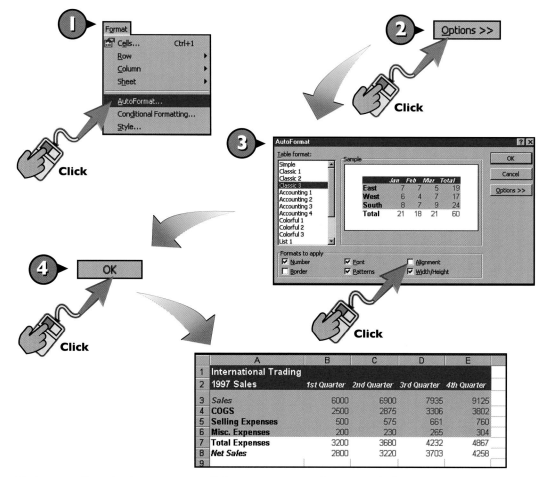

⊘ **Change Formatting after AutoFormat**
To change the cell formatting after an AutoFormat has been applied, select the cells whose formatting you want to change and choose **Format, Cells.** Select the desired formats in the Format Cells dialog box.

I ▶ Click any cell in the list or range of data you want to format and choose **Format, AutoFormat**.

2 ▶ Click the **Options** button in the AutoFormat dialog box. A group of format categories appears at the bottom of the dialog box.

3 ▶ Select the format you want to apply to your worksheet. Then click to deselect the check box next to any format category you don't want to apply.

4 ▶ Click **OK**. The modified Autoformat is applied.

Task 20: Wrapping Text in a Cell

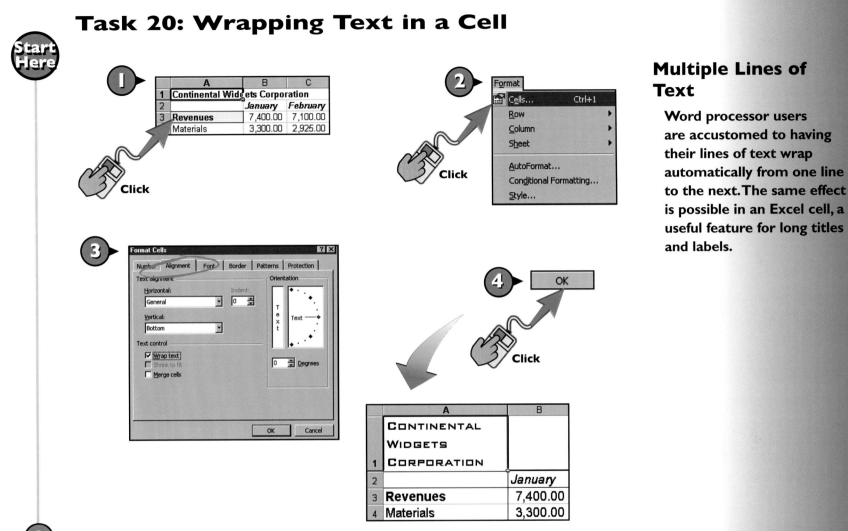

Multiple Lines of Text

Word processor users are accustomed to having their lines of text wrap automatically from one line to the next. The same effect is possible in an Excel cell, a useful feature for long titles and labels.

① Select the cell or range whose text you want to wrap.

② Choose **Format, Cells** to display the Format Cells dialog box.

③ On the Alignment tab, click the **Wrap Text** check box.

④ Click **OK** in the Format Cells dialog box. The row height automatically adjusts to display the wrapped text.

✓ **Column Width Impacts Wrapping**
If the text in the selected cell is not longer than the column width, text wrapping has no effect.

End Task

PART 6

Formulas and Functions

Formulas in Excel look like the formulas everyone is familiar with. For example, 2 + 2 equals 4 in Excel just as it does everywhere else. The only difference is that in Excel, formulas all begin with an equals sign, so you would type this one into your worksheet as **= 2 + 2**.

Even better, you wouldn't have to type it at all. Excel has dozens of built-in formulas, called *functions*, to take care of all the formula writing for you. Just insert your numbers, and Excel performs calculations from the simple to the complex with lightning speed.

When creating formulas in Excel, you use arithmetic operators including the symbols *, +, -, and / for multiplication, addition, subtraction, and division. The ^ (caret) character is used for exponentiation. Comparison operators include <, >, >=, and <= for less than, greater than, greater than or equal to, and less than or equal to.

Tasks

Task 1: Adding Numbers with AutoSum

Start Here

Instant Adding Machine

AutoSum automatically adds columns and rows of numbers. Excel then deposits the resulting sum (or total) in the selected cell.

1

6	Current Assets	
7	Cash	$ 26,500.00
8	Receivable	$ 27,561.00
9	Supplies	$ 14,323.00
10	Products in process	$ 7,700.00
11	Finished products	$ 8,410.00
12	*Total Current Assets*	$ 84,494.00
13		

Click

2 Σ

Click

✓ **Want to Cancel AutoSum?**
To back out of an AutoSum operation, press **Esc** instead of **Enter**.

3

6	Current Assets	
7	Cash	26,500.00
8	Receivable	$ 27,561.00
9	Supplies	$ 14,323.00
10	Products in process	$ 7,700.00
11	Finished products	$ 8,410.00
12	*Total Current Assets*	$ 84,494.00
13		=SUM(B7:B12

Click & Hold

✓ **The Formula Bar Holds the Formula**
The instant formula produced by AutoSum, in the form **=SUM(A1:A12)**, is actually Excel's **SUM** function, a kind of prefabricated formula. The formula doesn't appear in the cell itself, but is displayed on the Formula bar when the cell is selected.

4

B13	▼	= =SUM(B7:B12)
	A	**B**
1	*Shandy Enterprises Incorporated*	
2	*Statement of Financial Position*	
3	*December 31, 1995*	
4	*(Amounts in 000's of dollars)*	
5	**Assets**	
6	**Current Assets**	
7	Cash	$ 26,500.00
8	Receivable	$ 27,561.00
9	Supplies	$ 14,323.00
10	Products in process	$ 7,700.00
11	Finished products	$ 8,410.00
12	*Total Current Assets*	$ 84,494.00
13		168,988.00

⏎Enter

1 ▶ Select the cell that immediately follows the end of a column or row of numbers you want to total.

2 ▶ Click the **AutoSum** button on the Standard toolbar.

3 ▶ To change the selected range, point to the first cell in the new range, hold down the left mouse button, and drag to select the cells you want to total.

4 ▶ Press **Enter** to total the numbers and insert the sum in the cell selected in step 1.

End Task

Task 2: Subtracting Numbers

1

	A	B
1	Shandy Enterprises Incorporated	
2	Statement of Financial Position	
3	December 31, 1995	
4	(Amounts in 000's of dollars)	
5	Assets	
6	Current Assets	
7	Cash	$ 26,500.00
8	Receivable	$ 27,561.00
9	Supplies	$ 14,323.00
10	Products in process	$ 7,700.00
11	Finished products	$ 8,410.00
12	*Total Current Assets*	$ 84,494.00
13		168,988.00
14	Long Term Assets	
15	Plant and Equipment	$270,000.00
16	*Less: Allowance for depreciation*	$ 96,500.00
17	*Total Long Term Assets*	

Click

2 =

3

Click

COUNT ▼ X ✓ = =B15
? Formula result = $ 270,000.00   OK

2	Statement of Financial Position	
3	December 31, 1997	
4	(Amounts in 000's of dollars)	
5	Assets	
6	Current Assets	
7	Cash	$ 26,500.00
8	Receivable	$ 27,561.00
9	Supplies	$ 14,323.00
10	Products in process	$ 7,700.00
11	Finished products	$ 8,410.00
12	*Total Current Assets*	$ 84,494.00
13		
14	Long Term Assets	
15	Plant and Equipment	$ 270,000.00
16	*Less: Allowance for depreciation*	$ 96,500.00
17	*Total Long Term Assets*	=B15

4

COUNT ▼ X ✓ = =B15
? Formula result = $ 270,000.00

2	Statement of Financial Position	
3	December 31, 1997	
4	(Amounts in 000's of dollars)	
5	Assets	
6	Current Assets	
7	Cash	$ 26,500.00
8	Receivable	$ 27,561.00
9	Supplies	$ 14,323.00
10	Products in process	$ 7,700.00
11	Finished products	$ 8,410.00
12	*Total Current Assets*	$ 84,494.00
13		
14	Long Term Assets	
15	Plant and Equipment	$ 270,000.00
16	*Less: Allowance for depreciation*	$ 96,500.00
17	*Total Long Term Assets*	=B15

Click

15	Plant and Equipment	$270,000.00
16	*Less: Allowance for depreciation*	$ 96,500.00
17	*Total Long Term Assets*	$173,500.00
18		
19	Total Assets	

1 Select the cell where you want the result of the formula to appear.

2 Click the **Edit Formula** button on the Formula bar.

3 Select the first cell in your subtraction formula; a moving border appears around the selected cell, and the cell reference appears on the Formula bar.

4 Type the minus sign (–) and select the cell to be subtracted; then press **Enter**. The formula result appears in the selected cell.

Arithmetic in Excel

Subtracting in Excel is like subtracting with a calculator, except you use cell references instead of numbers. You'll find that Excel calculations are far more flexible and convenient than those you make with a calculator.

✓ **Change a Formula**
To change a formula, click the Formula bar and type the required changes. If cell references need to change, simply delete the old references and select the new ones.

✓ **Cell References Provide Automatic Updates**
When you calculate with cell references (rather than numbers) in formulas, Excel automatically updates your totals anytime you change the numbers in the referenced cells. You don't need to mess with the formula.

End Task

Page
95

Task 3: Multiplying and Dividing Numbers

More Excel Arithmetic

Creating Excel formulas with cell references rather than numbers makes worksheets highly flexible.

✓ **You Can Move the Formula Palette**
The *Formula palette* is the gray pop-up that appears just under the Formula bar when you click the **Edit Formula** button. If the Formula palette gets in your way, drag it to a new location.

✓ **Multiply and Divide Ranges**
You can use Excel's Array feature to multiply or divide ranges. To create an array, begin with two equal-sized ranges of data (make sure the ranges are the same size). Select the range where the results will be placed and create the formula, selecting the two ranges instead of single cells. Press **Ctrl+Shift+Enter**.

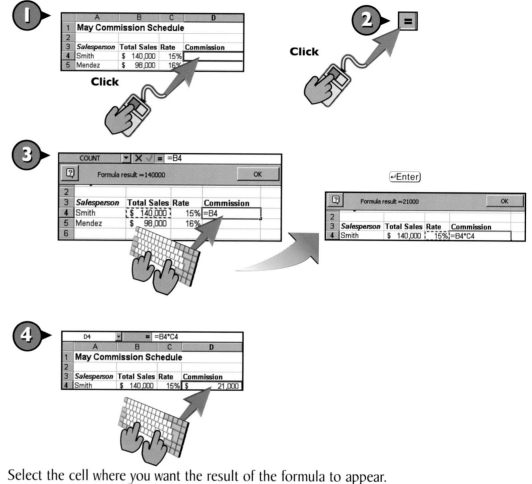

Start Here

Click

Click

1 ▶ Select the cell where you want the result of the formula to appear.

2 ▶ Click the **Edit Formula** button on the Formula bar.

3 ▶ Select the first cell in the formula; the cell reference appears on the Formula bar. Then type an asterisk (*****) to multiply or a forward slash (**/**) to divide.

4 ▶ Select the second cell in the formula; the cell reference appears on the Formula bar. Then press **Enter**. The result of the formula appears in the selected cell.

End Task

Task 4: Copying Formulas

Click

Click &
Hold

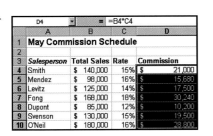

D4 =B4*C4

Apply One Formula to Many Cells

You can write one formula and apply it to many cells with a simple copy operation—another benefit of using cell references in Excel formulas.

✓ **Relative References Change When You Copy Formulas**
Formulas can be copied across ranges, because formula cell references are *relative references*. For example, if you create a formula in cell A3 that references cells A1 and A2, Excel interprets the reference as "use data from cells one row and two rows above this row."

✓ **Absolute References**
If a formula must refer to a specific cell even when you copy the formula to other locations, use an *absolute reference*. To convert a relative reference to an absolute reference, click the cell reference on the Formula bar and press F4.

 Click the cell containing a formula. (See Tasks 1, 2, and 3 for information about creating formulas.)

Point at the fill handle of the cell containing the formula. Then hold down the left mouse button and drag across the range of adjacent cells.

Release the mouse button, and the formula is copied to the selected range.

Task 5: Inserting Parentheses in Formulas

Build a More Complex Formula

By default, Excel calculates equations inside parentheses first, and then calculates equations using multiplication or division. Equations using addition or subtraction are calculated last. Anytime you mix different types of equations, you must use parentheses to indicate to Excel which calculations you want to do first.

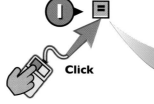

Click

	Automobile Costs, Per Mile	
2	**Automobile Costs, Per Mile**	
3	Total Costs:	5764
4	Less: Depreciation	675
5	Miles Driven:	11,345
6	Cost per Mile	=

IPMT ✕ ✓ = =

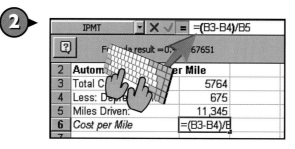

IPMT ✕ ✓ = =(B3-B4)/B5

Formula result = 0. 67651

2	**Autom er Mile**	
3	Total C	5764
4	Less: D	675
5	Miles Driven:	11,345
6	Cost per Mile	=(B3-B4)/B

↵Enter

3

B6 = =(B3-B4)/B5

	A	B	C
1			
2	**Automobile Costs, Per Mile**		
3	Total Costs:	5764	
4	Less: Depreciation	675	
5	Miles Driven:	11,345	
6	Cost per Mile	0.448568	
7			

 Missing Operators Produce Errors
Formulas missing an operator, such as a minus or plus sign, result in Excel error messages or errors such as #NAME? See Task 7 for information on troubleshooting formulas.

1 Select the cell where you want the result of the formula to appear. Then click the **Edit Formula** button on the Formula bar.

2 Type the formula on the Formula bar, adding parentheses where necessary. As you add the second parenthesis, Excel briefly displays the pair in boldface.

3 Press **Enter** to complete the formula.

 Start Here

 End Task

Task 6: Using Data from Multiple Worksheets in a Formula

Start Here

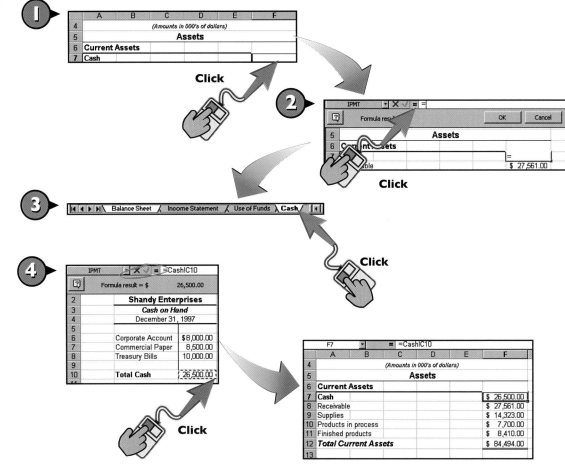

Click

Click

Click

Click

Click

Creating Summary Worksheets

Instead of scrolling back and forth between several worksheets or down vast distances of a single worksheet, keeping data in view on one worksheet can be very convenient. You can create simple formulas that can draw on data in many worksheets.

① Select the cell in the worksheet where you want the formula result to appear, sometimes referred to as the destination or target worksheet.

② Click the **Edit Formula** button on the Formula bar.

③ Click the worksheet tab of the worksheet where the data required for the formula is located, sometimes called the source worksheet.

④ Click the cell on the source worksheet containing the required data. Click the green check on the Formula bar to complete the formula and display the formula result.

✓ Use the Worksheet Name in a Cell Reference

Just as every cell on the worksheet has a unique reference, each cell in the entire workbook has a unique reference. Workbook references consist of the worksheet name followed by an exclamation point, so C10 in a worksheet called "Cash" has the workbook reference Cash!C10.

End Task

Task 7: Correcting Formula Errors

Repair Broken Formulas

If you make an error while entering a formula, Excel automatically suggests a correction you can accept or reject. If you make an error while you're editing an existing formula, you'll see error values such as #REF, #VALUE!, or #NAME!.

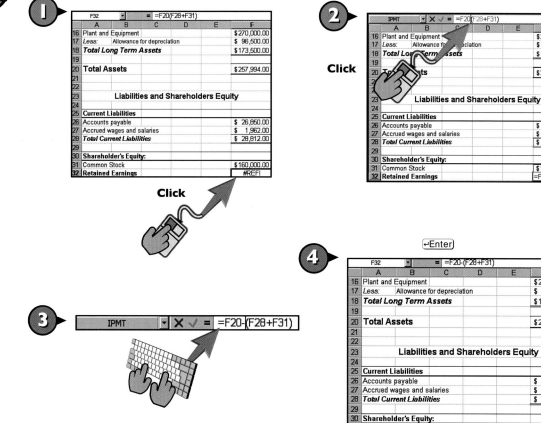

Click

Click

←Enter

Click

 Office Assistant Helps with Formula Errors
Type formula errors in the Office Assistant Search box and press Enter. The list of Help options displayed is a good starting point to learn more about error messages and how to prevent errors.

 You Can't Enter an Incorrect Formula
In most cases, Excel won't let you enter an incorrect formula; you have to fix the formula before Excel will accept it.

 Click the cell containing the error value.

 Click the **Formula** bar. Cell references are color-coded in the formula and in the cells themselves.

Type the missing operator (for example, a minus sign (–)).

Press **Enter** to complete the formula.

Task 8: Viewing Sums, Averages, and Counts with AutoCalculate

Start Here

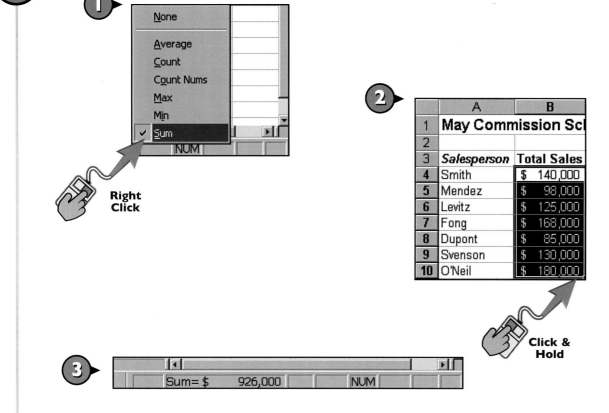

Right Click

Click & Hold

Sum= $ 926,000   NUM

AutoCalculate Gives Instant Results

When you just want to see a formula result without inserting it into a worksheet, select a range and glance at the result on the status bar. AutoCalculate can display the sum, the minimum and maximum values, the mean average, the number count, and the item count of a selected range. The default is the sum.

1 Right-click the status bar at the bottom of the Excel window and select the type of result you need from the shortcut menu.

2 Drag to select the range containing the data for which you want a result.

3 Read the result on the status bar.

✔ Counting Cells Based on Content

AutoCalculate's Count feature counts the number of non-blank cells in a selected range, including text. Count Nums counts the cells containing only numbers in a selected range.

Task 9: Working with Functions

Use Excel's Built-in Formulas

Functions are ready-made formulas for calculations of all kinds. You supply only your own data, because all of the formula-writing is done for you. Each Excel function begins with a function name, followed by the function components (called *arguments*) enclosed in parentheses. After you select a function, a pop-up called the *Formula palette* is displayed to walk you through the steps to complete the function.

Start Here

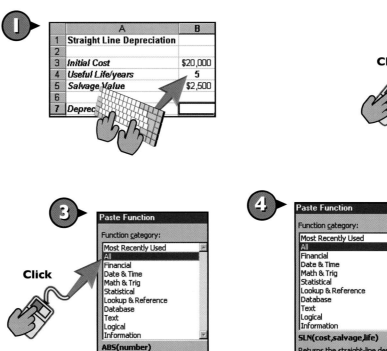

Click

Click

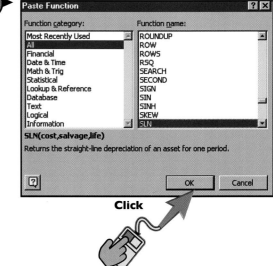
Click

 Use Cell References
Just as in creating formulas, use cell references rather than constant values as function arguments whenever possible. Using cell references enables you to update the numbers without having to rebuild the entire function.

1 Select the cell where you want the function result to appear.

2 Click the **Paste Function** button on the Standard toolbar.

3 Click a category in the Function Category list of the Paste Function dialog box, or choose **All** to see all of the functions.

4 Choose a function in the Function Name list. The function, its arguments, and a description appear at the bottom of the dialog box. Then click **OK**.

Next Step

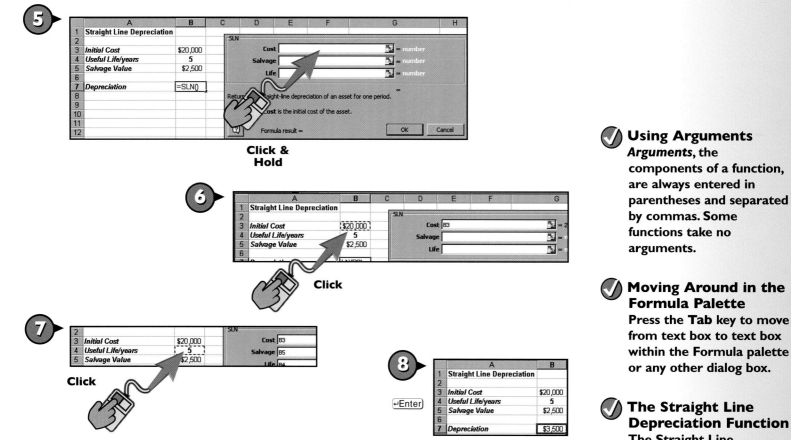

Click & Hold

Click

Click

←Enter

⑤ The Formula palette displays the selected function. If the Formula palette is in the way of the data, click and drag the palette out of the way.

⑥ Click the cell containing the data for the function's first argument. The cell reference appears in the argument's text box.

⑦ Click the second argument box in the Formula palette; then click the cell containing the data for the second argument. Repeat until all of the required arguments are entered.

⑧ Press **Enter** to insert the result in the worksheet.

✓ **Using Arguments**
Arguments, the components of a function, are always entered in parentheses and separated by commas. Some functions take no arguments.

✓ **Moving Around in the Formula Palette**
Press the **Tab** key to move from text box to text box within the Formula palette or any other dialog box.

✓ **The Straight Line Depreciation Function**
The Straight Line Depreciation (SLD) function shown in these steps calculates depreciation of an asset based on its initial cost, salvage (or sale) value, and years of useful life. The arguments are Cost, Salvage, and Life.

Task 10: Creating a Mortgage Payment Calculator

Start Here

Set Up Excel's Built-in Mortgage Calculator

PMT is the Excel function that calculates mortgage payments. Set up a worksheet to handle the loan variables, and use it with **PMT** to enjoy a flexible and powerful mortgage calculator.

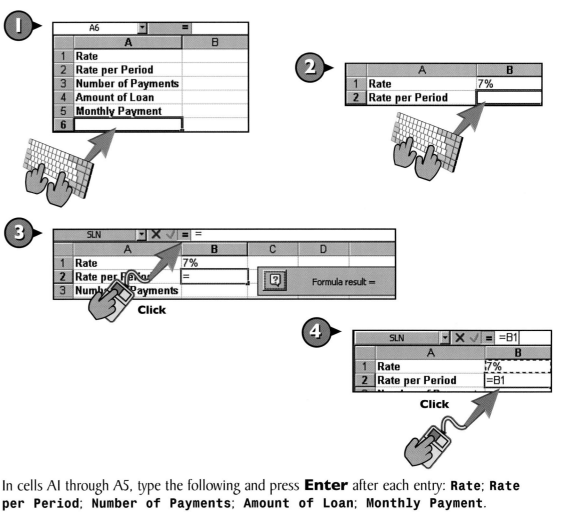

Click

Click

✓ **Compare Mortgages of Different Lengths**
If you are planning to evaluate mortgages of different lengths (15-year versus 30-year, for example), add another field to your mortgage calculator labeled "Number of Years." Create a formula for the Number of Periods field that multiplies the Number of Years field by 12 to keep your calculations on a per-period basis.

1. In cells A1 through A5, type the following and press **Enter** after each entry: `Rate`; `Rate per Period`; `Number of Payments`; `Amount of Loan`; `Monthly Payment`.

2. In cell B1, type the interest rate on the loan (for example, **7%**) and press **Enter**.

3. Select cell **B2** and click the **Edit Formula** button on the Formula bar. (Drag the Formula palette out of the way, as described in Task 9, step 5.)

4. Click cell **B1** to insert the cell reference in the formula.

Next Step

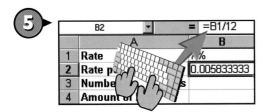

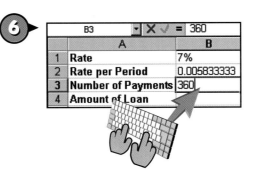

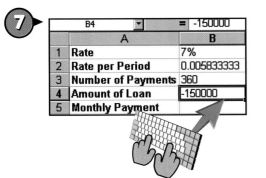

5 Type **/12** on the Formula bar and press **Enter**. Now any rate entered in B1 is automatically divided by 12 to display a monthly interest rate in B2.

6 Click cell **B3** and type the number of payments required by the loan. A 30-year loan requires 12 × 30 = 360 payments, for example, so type **360**.

7 Click cell **B4** and type a minus sign **(-)** followed by the loan amount (for example, **-150000**) and press **Enter**. (See Task 11 to put your mortgage calculator to work.)

End Task

Task 11: Calculating Mortgage Payments

Put the Mortgage Calculator to Work

In Task 10 you created the chassis for a mortgage calculator. With the addition of Excel's **PMT** function, the mortgage calculator gets an engine. The PMT function is used to calculate the payment on a loan, such as a mortgage.

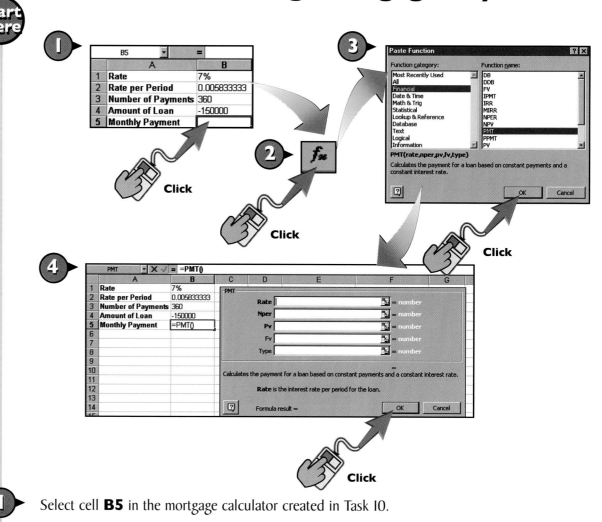

Start Here

1

	A	B
	B5	=
1	Rate	7%
2	Rate per Period	0.005833333
3	Number of Payments	360
4	Amount of Loan	-150000
5	Monthly Payment	

Click

2 f_{x}

Click

3 Paste Function

Function category:
Most Recently Used
All
Financial
Date & Time
Math & Trig
Statistical
Lookup & Reference
Database
Text
Logical
Information

Function name:
DB
DDB
FV
IPMT
IRR
MIRR
NPER
NPV
PMT
PPMT
PV

PMT(rate,nper,pv,fv,type)

Calculates the payment for a loan based on constant payments and a constant interest rate.

OK   Cancel

Click

4

	A	B	C	D	E	F	G
	PMT	=PMT()					
1	Rate	7%					
2	Rate per Period	0.005833333		PMT			
3	Number of Payments	360		Rate		= number	
4	Amount of Loan	-150000		Nper		= number	
5	Monthly Payment	=PMT()		Pv		= number	
6				Fv		= number	
7				Type		= number	
8							

Calculates the payment for a loan based on constant payments and a constant interest rate.

Rate is the interest rate per period for the loan.

Formula result =   OK   Cancel

Click

PMT Function Arguments

The format, or syntax, of the PMT function is identical to the syntax of most Excel functions. The function is followed by its arguments, in parentheses. There are five arguments for this function, but only the first three are required (these appear bold in the Formula palette): Rate (the monthly interest rate), **NPER** (the number of payment periods), and **PV** (the present value or amount of the loan).

1 Select cell **B5** in the mortgage calculator created in Task 10.

2 Click the **Paste Function** button on the Standard toolbar.

3 In the Paste Function dialog box, choose **Financial** in the Function Category list and choose **PMT** in the Function Name list. Then click **OK**.

4 Drag the Formula palette out of the way of your data.

Next Step

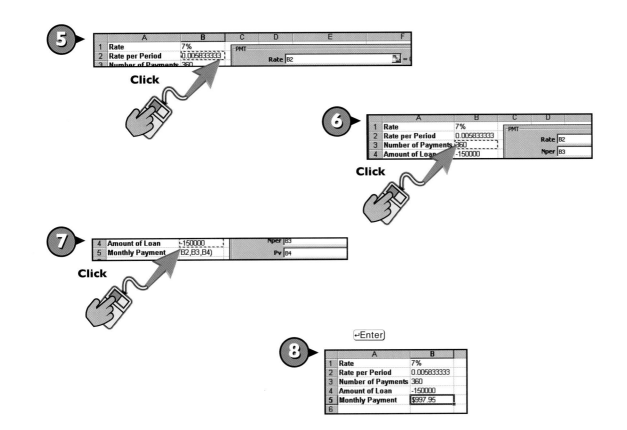

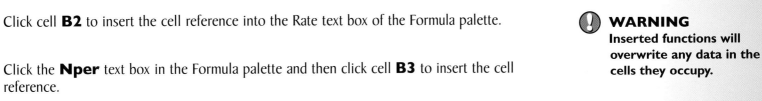

⏎Enter

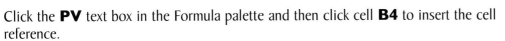

5 ▶ Click cell **B2** to insert the cell reference into the Rate text box of the Formula palette.

6 ▶ Click the **Nper** text box in the Formula palette and then click cell **B3** to insert the cell reference.

7 ▶ Click the **PV** text box in the Formula palette and then click cell **B4** to insert the cell reference.

8 ▶ Press **Enter** to insert the completed PMT function in cell B5.

⚠ **WARNING**
Inserted functions will overwrite any data in the cells they occupy.

End Task

Task 12: Inserting Averages

Average Results You Can Use

One of the most commonly used functions is the **AVERAGE** function. Use it to calculate average sales, average age—just about any average you can think of.

 WARNING
Cells containing zeros are included in the average calculation. Cells that are blank are not included.

 Use Ranges or Individual Cells as Arguments
You can use one range, several ranges, or individual cells as arguments for the **AVERAGE** function. When you need to specify multiple ranges or individual cell references, the Formula palette expands to accommodate up to 30 arguments.

The MEDIAN Function
To find the median of a range of values, use the **MEDIAN** function.

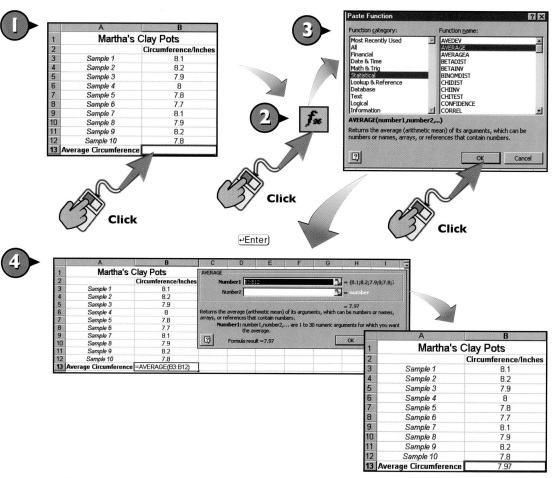

1 Click the cell where you want the AVERAGE function result to display.

2 Click the **Paste Function** button on the Standard toolbar.

3 In the Paste Function dialog box, choose **Statistical** in the Function Category list and choose **AVERAGE** in the Function Name list. Then choose **OK**.

4 Excel proposes a range to average in the Number I text box. If the range is correct, press **Enter**. If it isn't correct, select the correct range and press **Enter**.

Task 13: Calculating Days Between Dates

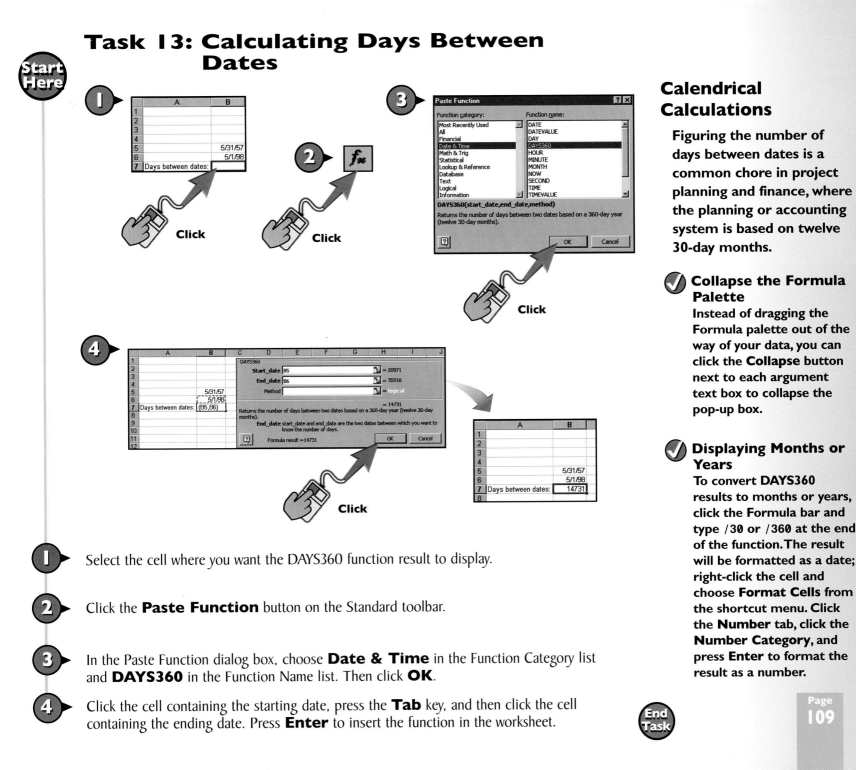

Start Here

1 Click

2 Click

3 Click

4 Click

Calendrical Calculations

Figuring the number of days between dates is a common chore in project planning and finance, where the planning or accounting system is based on twelve 30-day months.

✓ **Collapse the Formula Palette**
Instead of dragging the Formula palette out of the way of your data, you can click the **Collapse** button next to each argument text box to collapse the pop-up box.

✓ **Displaying Months or Years**
To convert DAYS360 results to months or years, click the Formula bar and type /30 or /360 at the end of the function. The result will be formatted as a date; right-click the cell and choose **Format Cells** from the shortcut menu. Click the **Number** tab, click the **Number Category,** and press **Enter** to format the result as a number.

1 Select the cell where you want the DAYS360 function result to display.

2 Click the **Paste Function** button on the Standard toolbar.

3 In the Paste Function dialog box, choose **Date & Time** in the Function Category list and **DAYS360** in the Function Name list. Then click **OK**.

4 Click the cell containing the starting date, press the **Tab** key, and then click the cell containing the ending date. Press **Enter** to insert the function in the worksheet.

End Task

Task 14: Calculating the Future Worth of a Savings Program

Are You Saving Enough?

The FV (Future Value) calculation can tell you how much your savings account will accumulate in a given number of years. The FV calculation works with any type of savings program in which you are setting aside a specific amount at regular intervals, such as $100 every month.

Use the FV calculation with any type of program, such as a 401k, an IRA, or even a savings account in a bank.

✓ FV Function Arguments

The FV function includes five arguments, but only the first three are required: **Rate** (the periodic interest rate), **NPER** (the number of payment periods), and **PMT** (the payment or amount of the contribution).

Start Here

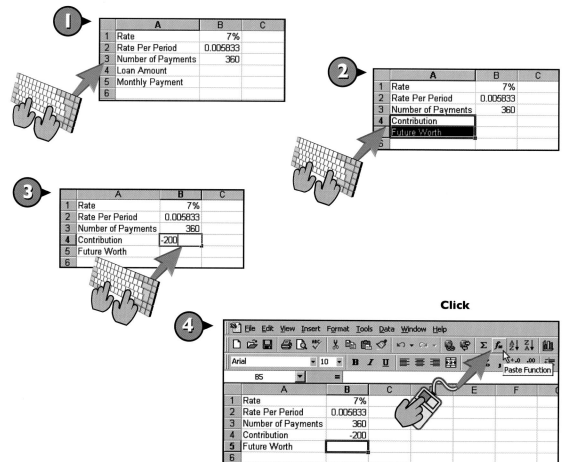

Click

1. Create the Mortgage Calculator. In cell B1, enter the interest rate you expect to receive on your savings program. In cell B3, enter the number of payments you expect to make.

2. Change Loan Amount (in cell A4) to **Contribution** and change Monthly Payment (in cell A5) to **Future Worth**.

3. Select cell **B4** and type a minus sign **(-)**, followed by the amount you contribute to the savings program; then press **Enter**. The amount must be entered as a negative number.

4. Select cell **B5** and then click the **Paste Function** button on the Standard toolbar.

Next Step

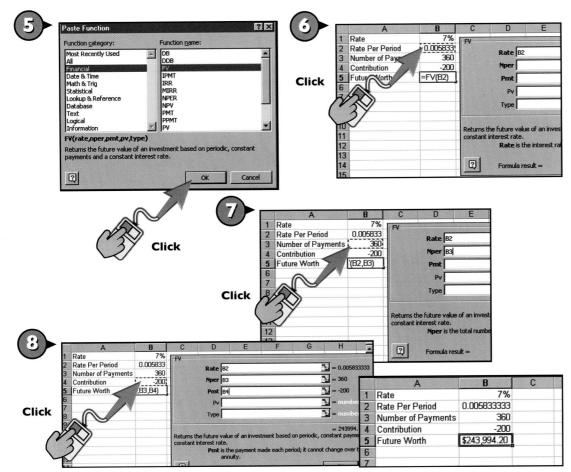

Calculating the Rate per Period

To determine the interest rate per period, divide the rate by the number of times per year you make the contributions. For example, if the interest rate is 10% and you are contributing once a month, the calculation would be =10%/12. If the interest rate is 10% and you are contributing every other week, the calculation would be =10%/26.

Calculating the Number of Payments

To determine the number of payments, multiply the years you will contribute by the number of times per year you make the contributions.

5 ► In the Paste Function dialog box, choose **Financial** from the Category list and **FV** from the Function Name list; then click **OK**.

6 ► Click cell **B2** to place the Rate Per Period cell reference in the RATE text box.

7 ► Click the **NPER** text box and click cell **B3**. The cell reference for the Number of Payments is added to the text box.

8 ► Click the **PMT** text box and click cell **B4**. The cell reference for the Contribution is added to the text box. Press **Enter** to display the Future Worth result in cell B5.

Printing Worksheets

Because word processors format text with the printed page in mind, printing pages is usually straightforward. Excel worksheets have a completely different approach to data. Worksheets can be as short as a line or two, or as long as a football field. Translating worksheets into printed pages, therefore, requires a little more effort.

But only a little more effort. A few extra steps produce clear and good-looking printouts from Excel worksheets.

Tasks

Getting Acquainted with Print Preview

Before printing any worksheet, you should use Excel's Print Preview feature to ensure the worksheet will be printed correctly.

✓ **Printing All Worksheets in a Workbook**
By default, only the active worksheet is printed. To print all worksheets in the workbook, choose **File, Print.** Then click **Entire Workbook** and choose **Preview.**

✓ **Printing Gridlines**
By default, worksheet gridlines do not print. To print the gridlines, click the **Setup** button in the Preview screen to display the Page Setup dialog box. Then select the Sheet tab and click **Gridlines.**

Task 1: Setting Up Your Worksheet by Using Print Preview

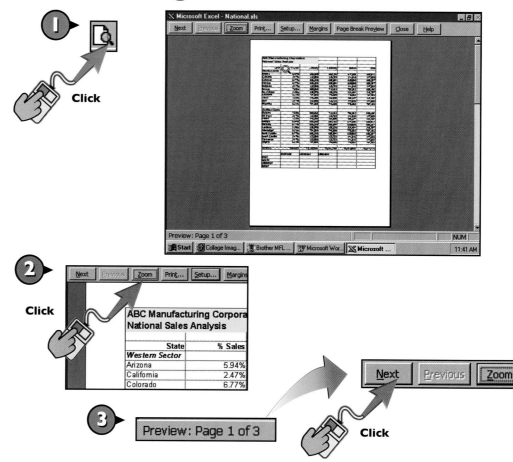

Click

Click

Click

Preview: Page 1 of 3

1 ▶ When you're ready to print, click the **Print Preview** button on the Standard toolbar. Print Preview displays the data from your active worksheet that will be on the first printed page.

2 ▶ Click the **Zoom** button to zoom in on the upper-left corner of the page, or click the mouse pointer on any part of the page to zoom into that area. Click again to zoom out.

3 ▶ Check the status bar in the Print Preview window to see how many pages you're about to print. Click the **Next** button or the **Previous** button on the Print Preview toolbar to view other pages.

Next Step

Page Setup dialog box

Page | Margins | Header/Footer | Sheet

Orientation
- A ● Portrait   A ○ Landscape

Scaling
- ● Adjust to: 100 ÷ % normal size
- ○ Fit to: 1 ÷ page(s) wide by 1 ÷ tall

Options...

Paper size: Letter 8 1/2 x 11 in
Print quality: 360 dpi
First page number: Auto

OK   Cancel

Print... | Setup... | Margins

Click

Print dialog box

Printer
Name: Brother MFC-7000 Series   Properties
Status: Idle
Type: Brother MFC-7000 Series
Where: BRMFC:
Comment: ☐ Print to file

Print range
- ● All
- ○ Page(s) From: ÷ To: ÷

Print what
- ○ Selection   ○ Entire workbook
- ● Active sheet(s)

Copies
Number of copies: 1 ÷
☑ Collate

Preview   OK   Cancel

Zoom | Print... | Setup...

Click

Click the **Setup** button on the Print Preview toolbar to display print options in the Page Setup dialog box.

Click the **Print** button on the Print Preview toolbar to display the Print dialog box and select the final print options. Choose **OK** to print or **Cancel** to exit the dialog box.

WARNING
Don't click the Print button on the Standard toolbar unless you have first established the print settings in the Print Preview screen. The Print button sends the worksheet to the printer immediately, giving you no opportunity to preview or change the default settings.

Changing the Print Margins
If just a small piece of the worksheet is printing on the last page, you can adjust the margins of the print area to change the print margins (see Task 2).

Task 2: Changing Printout Margins

Quick Margin Adjustments

For worksheets only slightly too wide or too long for an 8 1/2 by 11 page, margin adjustments are a quick fix.

Start
Here

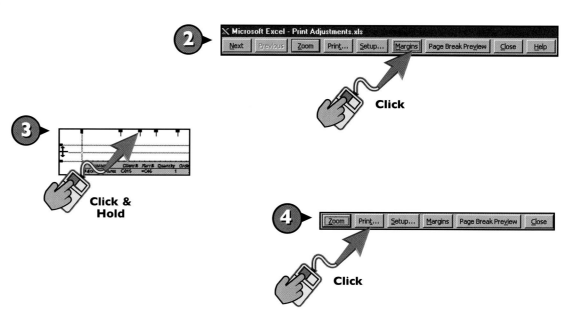

Click

Click

Click & Hold

Click

 Using Numerical Measurements

For exact margin adjustments to the fraction of an inch, click **Setup** on the Print Preview toolbar. Choose the **Margins** tab of the Page Setup dialog box, type the required margin settings in the text boxes, and click **OK**.

1. Click the **Print Preview** button on the Standard toolbar.

2. Click the **Margins** button on the Print Preview toolbar.

3. Point at any of the margin handles, hold down the left mouse button, and drag the margin handle to adjust.

4. After you adjust the margins to your satisfaction, click **Print** to print the worksheet.

End
Task

Task 3: Printing Selected Data

Start Here

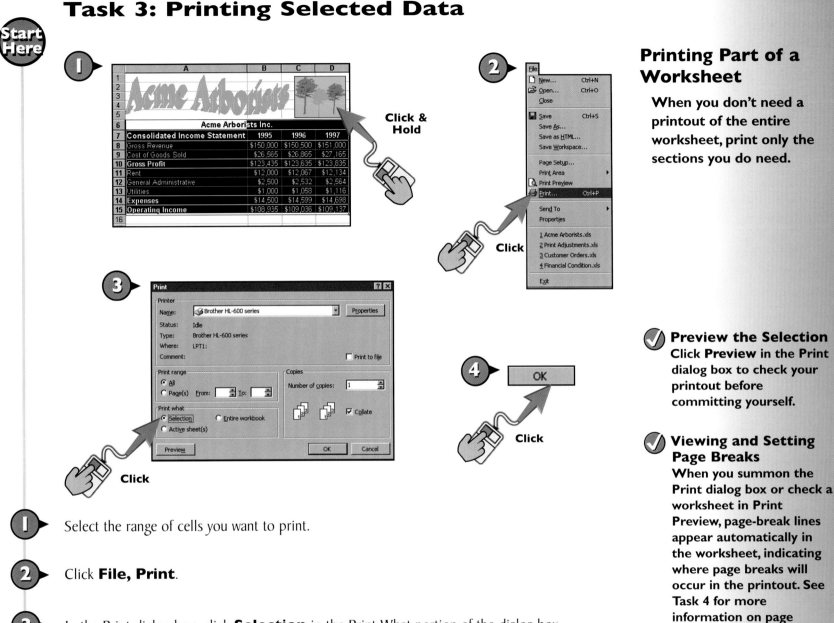

Click & Hold

Click

Click

Click

Printing Part of a Worksheet

When you don't need a printout of the entire worksheet, print only the sections you do need.

✓ **Preview the Selection**
Click **Preview** in the Print dialog box to check your printout before committing yourself.

✓ **Viewing and Setting Page Breaks**
When you summon the Print dialog box or check a worksheet in Print Preview, page-break lines appear automatically in the worksheet, indicating where page breaks will occur in the printout. See Task 4 for more information on page breaks.

1 ▶ Select the range of cells you want to print.

2 ▶ Click **File, Print**.

3 ▶ In the Print dialog box, click **Selection** in the Print What portion of the dialog box.

4 ▶ Click **OK** in the Print dialog box to print the selection.

End Task

Task 4: Adjusting Page Breaks

Controlling Where Excel Begins a Page

Page breaks are inserted automatically by Excel, based on your margin and paper size settings. Using Page Break Preview, you can view page breaks, move them, and insert your own. In Page Break Preview, page breaks are displayed as blue dashed lines; blue solid lines indicate the right and left margins.

✓ Automatic Versus Manual Page Breaks

Although you can move the automatically inserted page breaks, you can't remove them. The Insert, Remove Page Break command removes only manually inserted page breaks.

✓ Accessing Page Break Preview

In addition to using the View, Page Break Preview command, you can access the Page Break Preview from the Print Preview window.

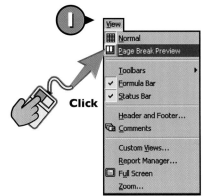

Click

Click & Hold

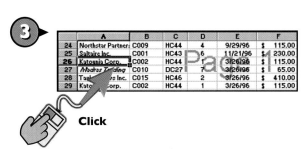

Click

> **1** Choose **View, Page Break Preview**.

> **2** Point at the dashed page-break line, hold down the left mouse button, and drag the line left or right, up or down, to break the page at a different spot on the worksheet.

> **3** To insert a horizontal page break, click the numbered row heading to be the first row on a new page. For a vertical break, click the alphabetical column heading.

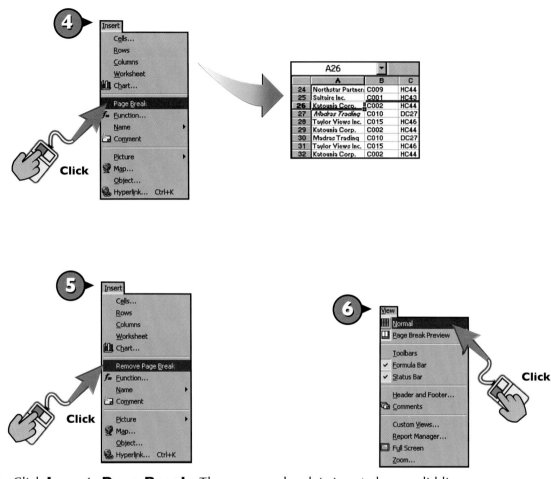

4 ▶ Click **Insert, Page Break**. The new page break is inserted as a solid line immediately above (or to the left of) the selected heading.

5 ▶ To remove a manually inserted page break, click any cell below a horizontal page break or to the right of a vertical page break. Then click **Insert, Remove Page Break**.

6 ▶ To exit Page Break Preview, click **View, Normal**.

✓ **Removing All Manually Inserted Page Breaks**
Click the gray button at the intersection of the alphabetical column heading and numerical row numbers to select the entire worksheet. Then choose **Insert, Reset All Page Breaks**.

Task 5: Adding Headers and Footers

Page Numbers and Other Printing Essentials

If you need page numbers, the filename, or the author's name to appear on your printed worksheets, add them in headers and footers. Headers and footers are printed at the top and bottom of every page of the printout, and you can customize them to suit your needs.

✅ **Customizing Headers and Footers**
For custom headers and footers, see Task 6.

✅ **Zoom In to Preview Headers and Footers**
To see your header and footer magnified, use the mouse to zoom in on them in the Print Preview window. Click again to restore the prior magnification.

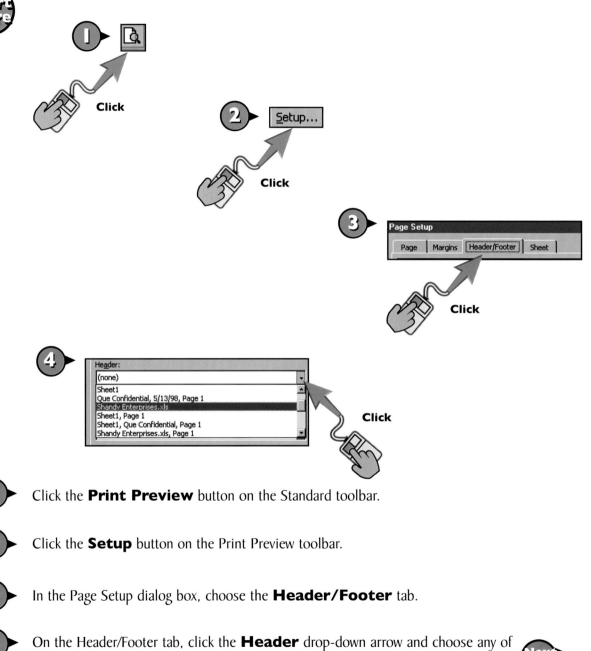

Click

Click

Click

Click

Start Here!

② Setup...

③ Page Setup
Page | Margins | Header/Footer | Sheet

④ Header:
(none)
Sheet1
Que Confidential, 5/13/98, Page 1
Shandy Enterprises.xls
Sheet1, Page 1
Sheet1, Que Confidential, Page 1
Shandy Enterprises.xls, Page 1

① Click the **Print Preview** button on the Standard toolbar.

② Click the **Setup** button on the Print Preview toolbar.

③ In the Page Setup dialog box, choose the **Header/Footer** tab.

④ On the Header/Footer tab, click the **Header** drop-down arrow and choose any of the headers on the menu.

Next Step

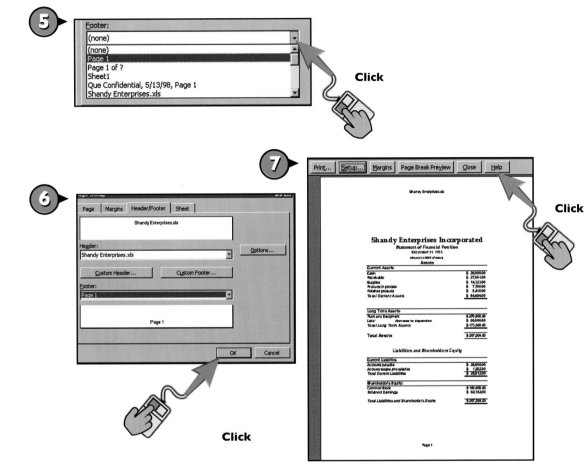

5 ▶ Click the **Footer** drop-down arrow and choose any of the footers on the menu.

6 ▶ The Preview areas on the Header/Footer tab show you how the header and footer will appear on each printed page. If your headers and footers look good, click **OK**.

7 ▶ Click **Close** on the Page Preview toolbar to exit Page Preview, or click **Print** to print the worksheet.

Headers and Footers Are Permanent
Headers and footers are added to the active worksheet only. After you add headers or footers to a worksheet, they print each time the worksheet is printed.

More on Headers and Footers

Excel includes several useful codes most people use for headers and footers, such as the date the worksheet was printed or the name of the worksheet tab. Additionally, you can type in virtually any text you choose. You can also specify the placement of the header and footer and use multiple lines with custom headers and footers.

Built-in Header and Footer Codes

Excel provides six codes you can insert, which are interpreted when you print the worksheet. Print codes begin with an ampersand (&) symbol. The codes are the current page number, total page count, date printed, time printed, workbook name, and worksheet name.

Task 6: Customizing Headers and Footers

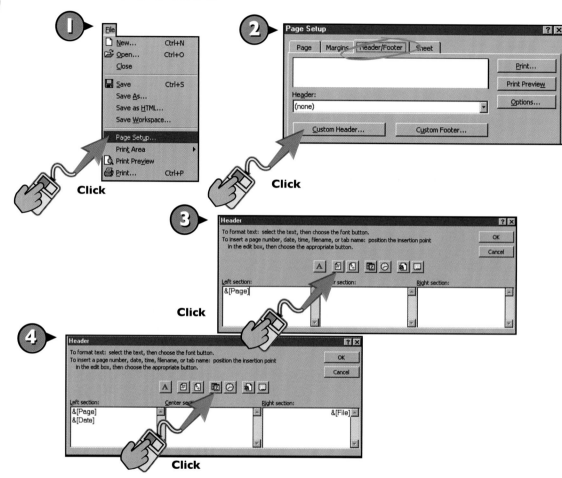

Click

Click

Click

Click

Click **File, Page Setup**.

On the Header/Footer tab of the Page Setup dialog box, click either **Custom Header** or **Custom Footer**.

To insert the built-in code that displays the page number, click in the desired alignment section and then click the second button. The &Page code is added to the section.

To insert a code that displays the printing date, click in the desired alignment section and then click the fourth button. The &Date code is added to the section.

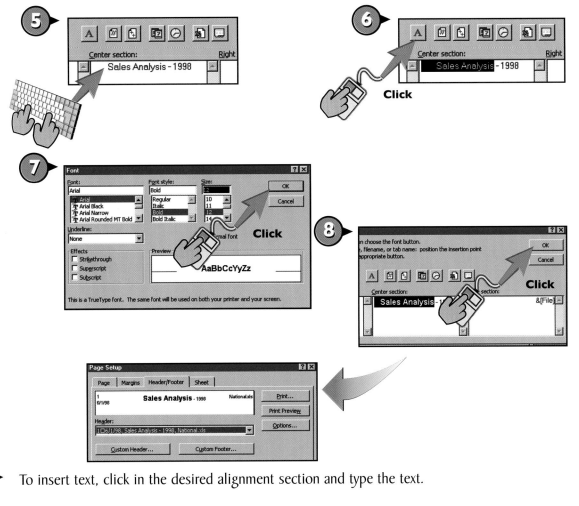

Click

Click

Click

To insert text, click in the desired alignment section and type the text.

To format text or built-in codes, hold down the left mouse button and highlight the text or code you want to format. Then click the **Font** button.

The Font dialog box displays. Change the font type, style, or size. When you finish, click **OK**.

Click **OK** to see how the custom header or footer will look.

Multiple Lines of Headers or Footers
Press **Enter** in an alignment section box to start a new line for a header or footer.

Getting Help
For more information about any of the buttons in the Header or Footer dialog box, click the question mark in the upper-right corner of the dialog box and then click the button.

Task 7: Printing Wide Worksheets

Changing the Print Orientation

Excel can print worksheets in *portrait orientation* (with the longer edges of the page at the left and right) or *landscape orientation* (with the longer edges of the page at the top and bottom). If your worksheet is wider than it is tall, print it in landscape orientation.

 Orientation Change Affects the Active Worksheet

By default, Excel prints in Portrait orientation. Choosing landscape for the active worksheet won't change the page orientation of the other worksheets in the workbook.

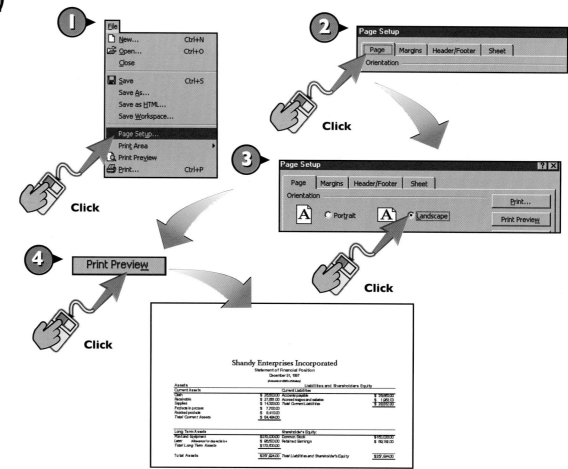

 ❶ Click **File, Page Setup**.

❷ Choose the **Page** tab of the Page Setup dialog box.

❸ Click **Landscape** to print wide worksheets across, rather than down the printed page.

❹ Click **Print Preview** in the Page Setup dialog box to see how the printout will look.

Task 8: Resizing Worksheets to Fit a Page Count

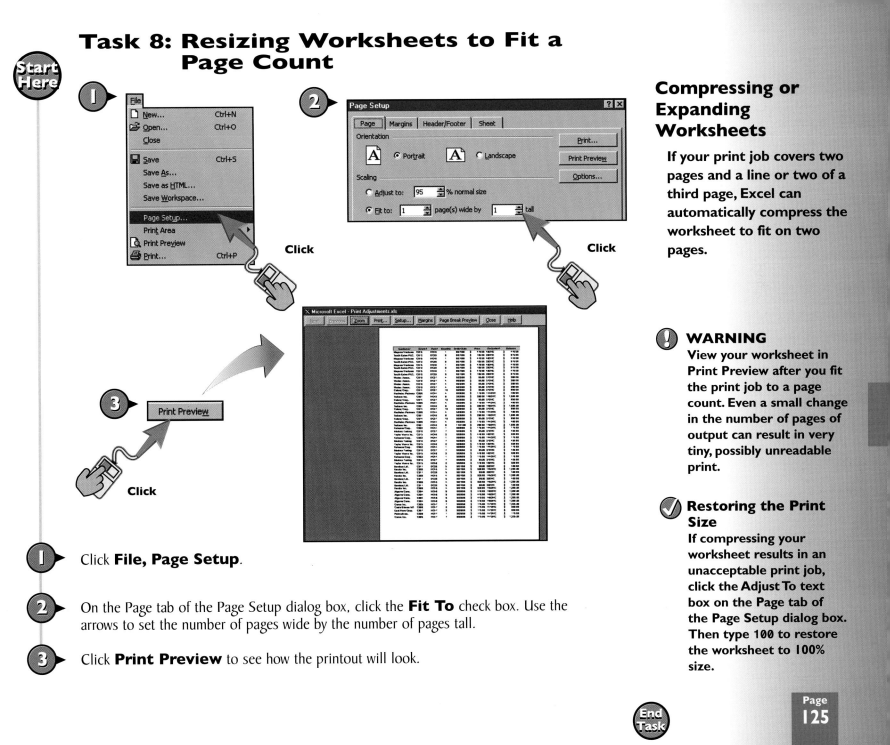

Compressing or Expanding Worksheets

If your print job covers two pages and a line or two of a third page, Excel can automatically compress the worksheet to fit on two pages.

WARNING

View your worksheet in Print Preview after you fit the print job to a page count. Even a small change in the number of pages of output can result in very tiny, possibly unreadable print.

Restoring the Print Size

If compressing your worksheet results in an unacceptable print job, click the Adjust To text box on the Page tab of the Page Setup dialog box. Then type 100 to restore the worksheet to 100% size.

1. Click **File, Page Setup**.

2. On the Page tab of the Page Setup dialog box, click the **Fit To** check box. Use the arrows to set the number of pages wide by the number of pages tall.

3. Click **Print Preview** to see how the printout will look.

Task 9: Printing Column or Row Titles on All Pages

Column and Row Titles on Every Page

If your worksheet is a long list with labeled columns or rows, set up the print job so pages print with their column or row titles on every page.

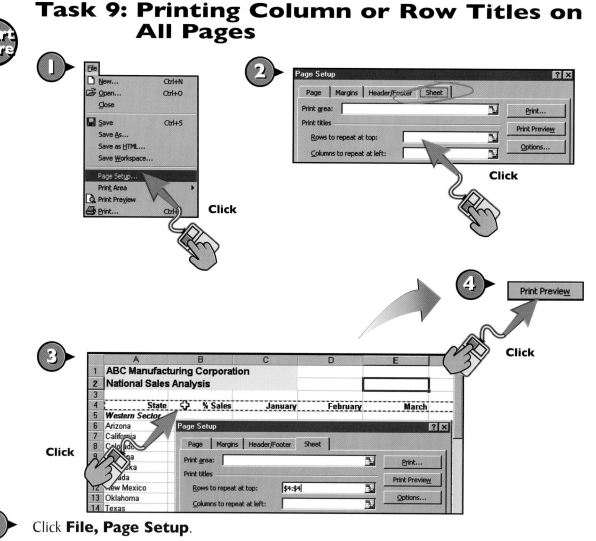

Repeating Row Labels
If your repeated titles are arranged vertically in a column, choose **Columns to Repeat at Left** in the Page Setup dialog box.

1 Click **File, Page Setup**.

2 Click the **Sheet** tab of the Page Setup Dialog box. To display column titles that appear in a specific row, click in the **Rows to Repeat at Top** text box.

3 Select any cell in the row containing the column titles you want repeated on every page. You may need to drag the dialog box out of your way.

4 Click **Print Preview** in the Page Setup dialog box to see how the titles will appear on the printed pages.

Task 10: Centering Data on the Page

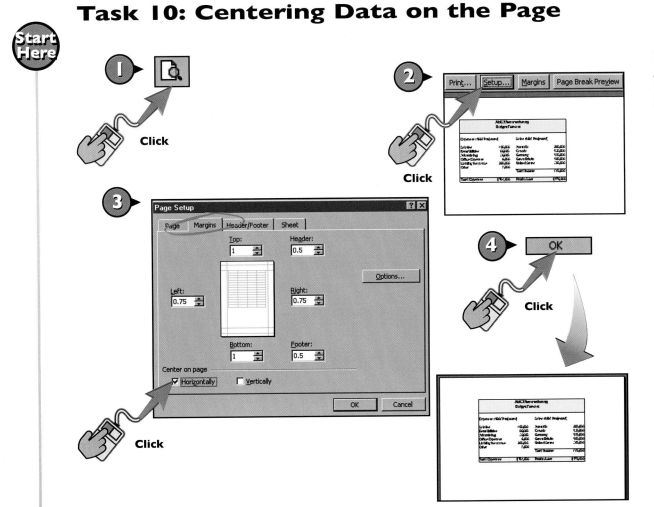

Click

Click

Click

Click

OK

Centering Output for Attractive Printouts

Each page is printed so the data starts in the upper-left corner of the page. It is often more attractive to center the data horizontally, vertically, or both.

1. Click the **Print Preview** button on the Standard Toolbar.

2. Notice how the worksheet is oriented to start printing in the upper-left corner of the page. Click **Setup** to display the Page Setup dialog box.

3. Click the **Margins** tab of the Page Setup dialog box, and click **Horizontally** or **Vertically** (or both) to change how the data is centered on the page.

4. Click **OK** to see the changes in the Print Preview screen.

✓ **Centering Affects Printing Only**
Changing placement of the printed data merely changes where the data is printed on the page. The alignment of the data within the worksheet cells is not affected.

End Task

Creating Charts

Charts, which you might also know as graphs, give you a bird's-eye view of data. Like a window on a high floor overlooking a crowded city, a chart lets you see the entire worksheet at a glance. In a single colorful picture, a good chart can summarize and illuminate a sea of numbers.

Excel has a selection of charts for every type of data. Excel charts are also very customizable. Although every part of a chart can be changed as needed, most Excel charts are perfectly serviceable just as they are. Part 8 looks at creating and editing insightful charts.

Tasks

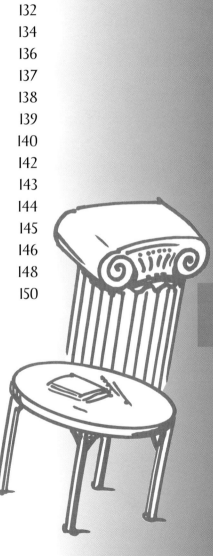

Task 1: Learning the Parts of Excel Charts

The Language of Excel Charts

Understanding the parts of Excel charts is like learning a new language—before you can converse effectively, you have to know what to call everything!

Start Here

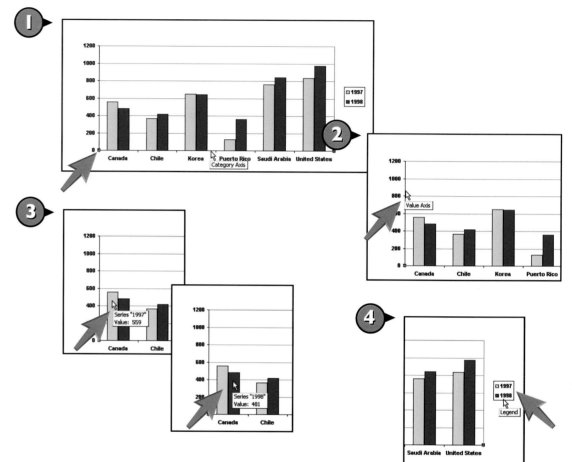

✓ Excel's Default Chart Type
The default chart created by Excel is the two-dimensional column chart seen in the figures here.

✓ Chart ScreenTips
Point to any part of a chart and Excel displays a ScreenTip identifying the chart component.

1 The horizontal line at the bottom of a chart is called an axis. Point to the horizontal line to determine if it is the **category axis**.

2 The vertical line at the left of a chart is also called an axis. Point to the vertical line to determine if it is the **value axis**.

3 The group of colored columns represents a **data series**. Point to one of the columns to identify the series. A ScreenTip also identifies the value for the specific column.

4 A **legend** usually appears on the right side of a chart to identify the series of data being plotted.

Next Step

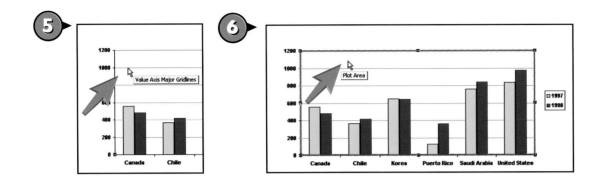

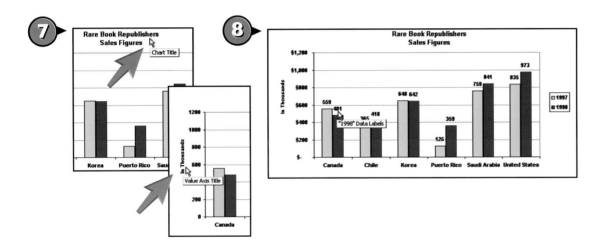

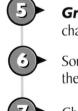

5 *Gridlines* that intersect the value axis help to identify the numbers being plotted on the chart.

6 Sometimes it is necessary to enlarge or shrink the chart plot area. To make sure you select the plot area, position the mouse pointer between the gridlines and look for the ScreenTip.

7 Chart and axis titles can be added to your charts. Titles help you (and others) understand what data is being plotted in the chart.

8 To show the specific numbers being plotted, add data labels to your chart.

 Value Axis Versus Category Axis
Distinguishing between the value axis and the category axis is easy. The axis that displays the numerical data being graphed is always the value axis. In the figures here, the value axis is the vertical axis.

 Data Series
The legend identifies the data series in a chart.

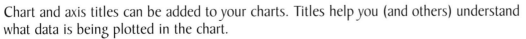

Task 2: Creating a Quick Column Chart

Charts in a Hurry

You can take a lot of time over an Excel chart, adjusting every detail from the colors to the shape of the various **chart objects**. You can also produce a useful chart in just a moment or two.

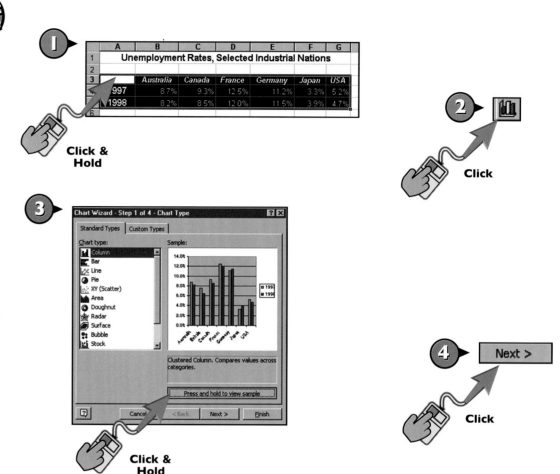

Click & Hold

Click

Click & Hold

Click

Click

✅ Categories, Values, and Series

In the chart shown here, the categories are seven nations and the values are the unemployment rates in each nation. The two data series are 1997 and 1998.

✅ Embedded Charts Versus Chart Sheets

Charts can be placed either on an existing worksheet or on a new worksheet devoted to just the chart. Charts placed on an existing worksheet are referred to as embedded charts. Charts placed on their own worksheets are referred to as **chart sheets**.

1 ▶ Select the data you want to chart, including column and row titles. If your worksheet data has a title, do not include the title in the selection.

2 ▶ Click the **Chart Wizard** button on the Standard toolbar.

3 ▶ In step 1 of the Chart Wizard, the default selection is a column chart. Hold the left mouse button on the **Press and Hold to View Sample** button to preview your chart.

4 ▶ Click **Next** to proceed to step 2 of the Chart Wizard.

Next Step

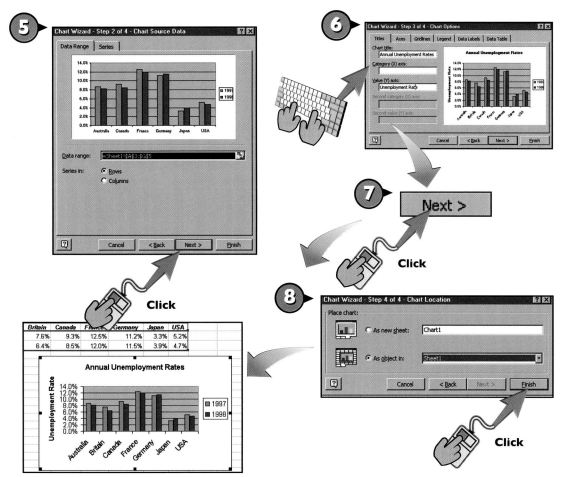

5 ▶ Step 2 of the wizard is verifying you selected the correct range of data in the worksheet. Additionally, you have the option to plot the worksheet data by rows or columns. Click **Next**.

6 ▶ Step 3 of the wizard invites you to add titles for the chart and axes, if you want them. The preview window updates to reflect the titles you type.

7 ▶ Click **Next** to proceed to the final step of the Chart Wizard.

8 ▶ In step 4 of the wizard, you can choose to place the chart on a new sheet or on an existing sheet. Click **Finish** to complete the wizard and place the chart.

✔️ **Deleting Charts**
To delete an embedded chart, click the chart and press **Delete**. To delete a chart sheet, right-click the sheet tab and choose **Delete**.

Task 3: Selecting Chart Types

Charts for Every Occasion

Excel has 14 standard chart types, and each chart type has several subtypes for you to choose from. Many of the chart types have both two-dimensional and three-dimensional options. Choosing among the other variations depends on the nature of your data.

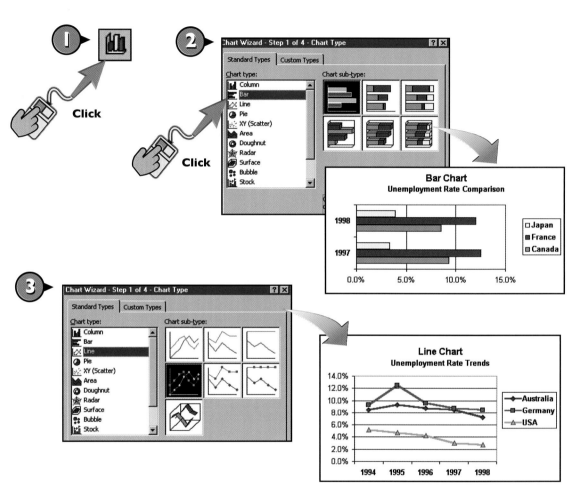

Bar Chart
Unemployment Rate Comparison

Line Chart
Unemployment Rate Trends

✓ Understanding the Chart Subtypes

When you click a chart subtype, a description appears directly below the subtype options.

✓ Change the Type of an Existing Chart

Click an embedded chart, or click the worksheet tab of a chart sheet. Then click the **Chart Wizard** button on the Standard toolbar. Choose a different chart type and click **Finish** to instantly switch chart types.

1 ▶ Click the **Chart Wizard** button on the Standard toolbar to display Step 1 of 4 – Chart Type.

2 ▶ Click **Bar** on the Chart Type menu. With bar charts, the category axis becomes vertical and the value axis is laid out horizontally.

3 ▶ Use line charts when you have a lot of data to plot. Line charts are good at illustrating trends over a period of time. Click **Line** on the Chart Type menu.

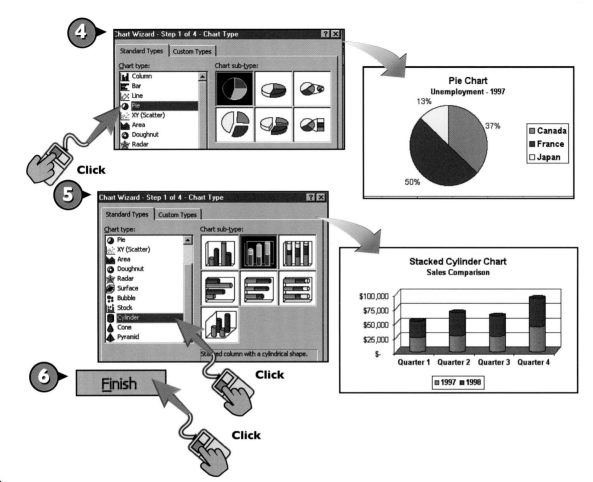

4 ▶ Pie charts show how each item or part relates to the whole by answering "How much of the whole is this part?" Click **Pie** on the Chart Type menu.

5 ▶ A stacked chart, available with column and bar charts, is used to show the cumulative total of the **data points**. Click the chart type and then select the stacked subtype.

6 ▶ After you select the chart type and subtype you want to use, proceed through the remaining steps, as described in Task 2. Click **Finish** to create the chart.

✅ **Column/Bar Variations**
Three exciting alternatives to column or bar charts are the cylinder, cone, and pyramid chart types.

Fitting Embedded Charts on the Worksheet

When you create a chart in Excel, you have the option of selecting where the chart will be placed. Charts placed next to the worksheet data are called embedded charts. These charts can be resized and moved around the worksheet.

✓ Identifying Chart Objects

Charts are composed of various objects and areas, each with a name. Point within a chart at any of the chart objects or areas to see a ScreenTip with the object or area name. The name also appears in the *Name Box*, to the left of the Formula bar.

Task 4: Moving and Resizing Embedded Charts

Start Here

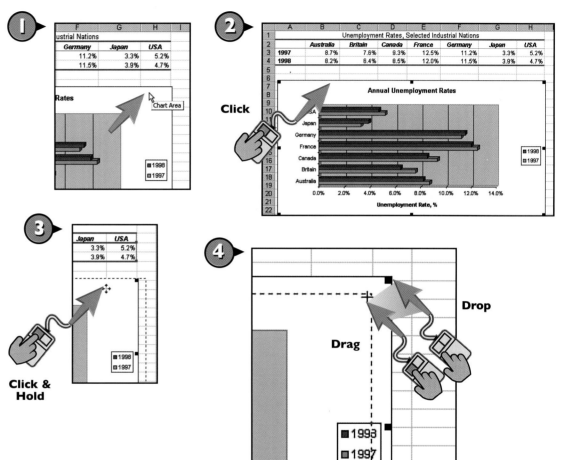

Click

Click & Hold

Drag

Drop

 Point inside the chart near the chart's outer edge. A ScreenTip labeled Chart Area appears.

2 Click to select the chart area. **Selection handles** appear around the chart area.

3 To move a chart, position the mouse pointer inside the chart area, away from the chart objects. Hold down the left mouse button and drag the chart to a new location.

4 To resize a chart, point at one of the four corner selection handles and hold down the left mouse button. Drag inward to reduce the chart size or outward to enlarge it.

End Task

Task 5: Resizing Chart Sheet Charts

Start Here

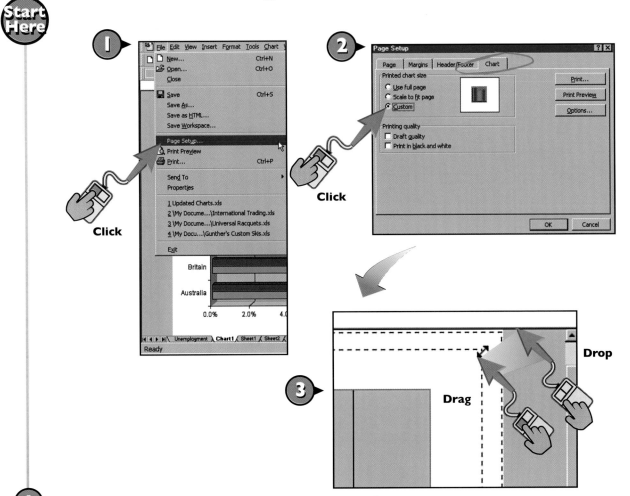

Click

Click

Drag

Drop

Smaller Chart Sheet Charts

Charts placed on their own worksheets are called chart sheets. A chart sheet contains only one chart and is linked to the worksheet that contains the data plotted in the chart. If you need a smaller chart (for insertion into a Word document, for example, or for a smaller printout), chart sheet charts can be resized.

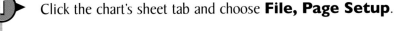

1. Click the chart's sheet tab and choose **File, Page Setup**.

2. On the Chart tab of the Page Setup dialog box, click **Custom** and choose **OK**.

3. Click the chart and point at one of the corner selection handles. Hold down the left mouse button and drag inward to reduce the size of the chart.

✓ Changing the Chart Location

To convert a chart sheet to an embedded chart in a worksheet, select the chart and choose **Chart, Location**. In the Chart Location dialog box, click the **As Object In** option button. Click the drop-down arrow and choose the worksheet in which you want the chart embedded; then click **OK**.

Task 6: Selecting Chart Objects

Preparing for Chart Alterations

An Excel chart is like a room full of furniture. Objects in the chart can be moved, recolored, and removed. To effect any alterations, objects must be selected first.

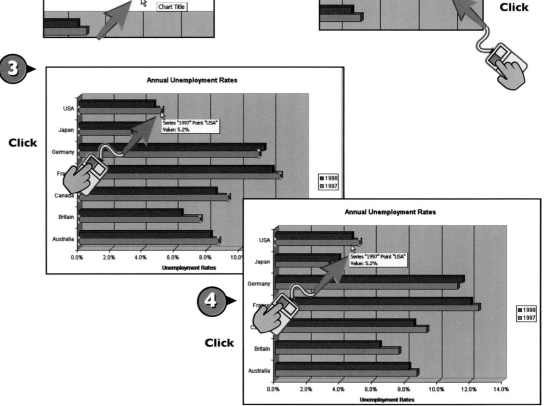

 Deselecting Objects
To cancel any selection, press the **Esc** key.

 Understanding Data Points
Data series are composed of data points, which correspond to the individual worksheet cells containing the values on which the chart is based.

1 Point at the area or object within the chart you want to select (for example, the **Chart Title**); note the area or object name on the ScreenTip that accompanies the mouse pointer.

2 Click to select the object. Selection handles appear around the object.

3 Click a data series to select it (for example, the **1997** series). Selection handles appear around each data point in the series.

4 To select an individual data point, first click the data series. Then click the data point. Selection handles appear only around the selected data point.

Task 7: Editing Chart Data

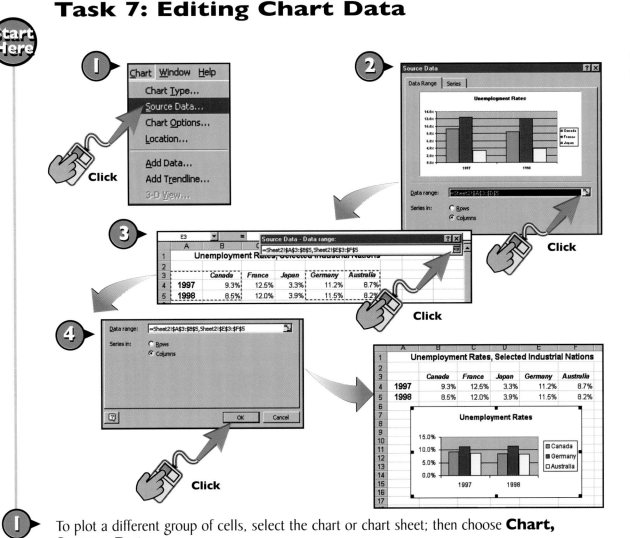

Changing the Data Being Plotted

You can make two types of changes regarding the chart data: You can edit the data in the worksheet cells or you can select different cells to plot.

✓ **Editing Worksheet Data**

To edit the data in the worksheet cells, select the cell containing the data you want to change and type the new data. When you press **Enter**, the chart immediately plots the new data.

✓ **Selecting Nonadjacent Cells**

To select nonadjacent cells, select the first group of cells. Then press and hold **Ctrl** as you select the remaining groups of cells.

1 To plot a different group of cells, select the chart or chart sheet; then choose **Chart, Source Data**.

2 The Source Data dialog box displays, with the cells currently being plotted listed in the Data Range edit box. Click the **Collapse** button to reduce the size of the dialog box.

3 Select the cells you want to plot, including the column and row titles. The **Collapse** button has become an **Expand** button; click it to expand the Source Data dialog box.

4 The Source Data dialog box now shows the new cells plotted in the chart. Click **OK** and the chart in the worksheet reflects the new data.

End Task

Altering Chart Appearance

You can change the colors or apply patterns to add visual interest to a chart. Charts destined for black-and-white printers benefit especially from contrasting colors and pattern changes.

Task 8: Formatting Chart Object Colors and Patterns

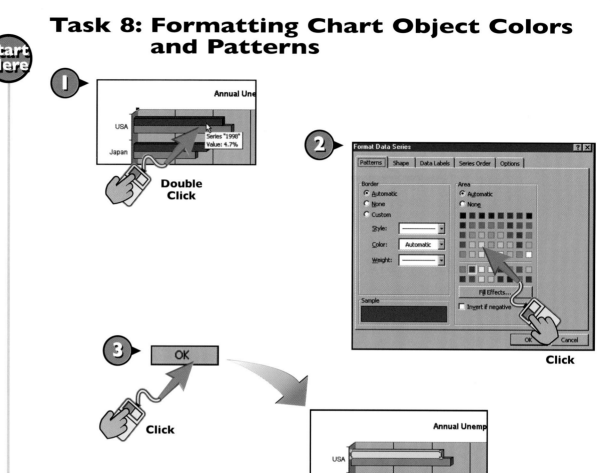

Double Click

Click

Click

✓ **Formatting Data Points**

To format individual data points, click a data point twice (two separate clicks) to select it. Then double-click the data point to display the Format dialog box.

✓ **Formatting 3D Charts**

Three-dimensional charts have walls and floors that can be recolored. Double-click them to display the Format dialog box.

① To change the color of a chart object, double-click the chart object. The Format dialog box appears.

② On the **Patterns** tab, click an **Area Color** to recolor the selected chart object.

③ Click **OK** in the Format dialog box; the color change is applied to the object.

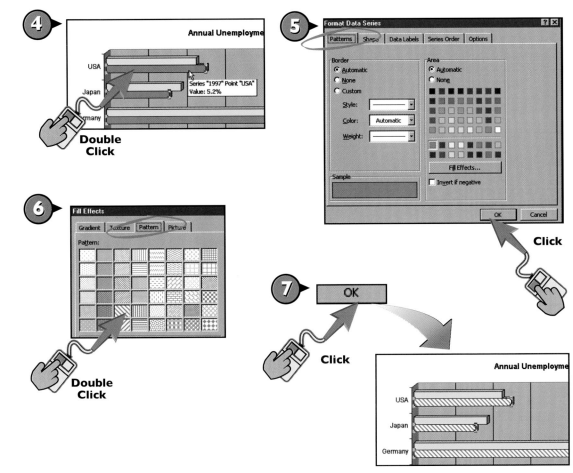

Additional Formatting Options

Explore the Gradient and Texture tabs of the Fill Effects dialog box for more chart-formatting choices.

Using Pictures Instead of Patterns

To replace data series objects such as columns or bars with a picture, double-click the data series and choose **Pattern, Fill Effects**. Choose the **Picture** tab of the Fill Effects dialog box and click **Select Picture**. Browse your folders or clip art for the picture you need and double-click to select it. Click **OK** in the Fill Effects and Format dialog boxes.

④ To apply a pattern to a chart object, double-click the chart object; the Format dialog box appears.

⑤ On the **Patterns** tab in the Format dialog box, click **Fill Effects**.

⑥ Click the **Pattern** tab of the Fill Effects dialog box and double-click the pattern you want to apply to the object. The Fill Effects dialog box disappears.

⑦ Click **OK** in the Format dialog box; the pattern is applied to the chart object.

Task 9: Editing Chart and Axis Titles

Rewriting and Reformatting Chart Titles

Changing the wording and fonts of chart and axis titles is a matter of pointing and clicking—carefully. Two single clicks are used to edit title text, and a double-click to change fonts.

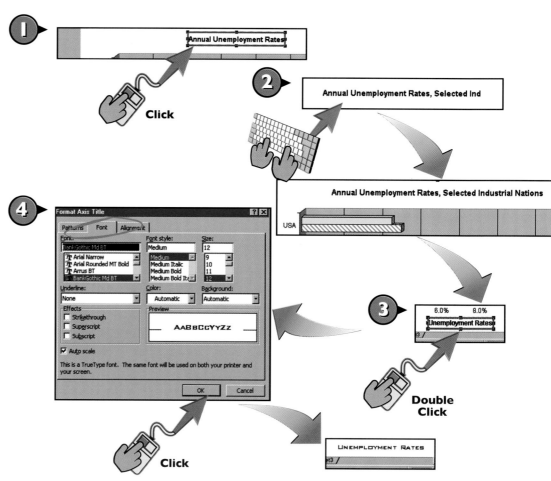

✓ **Deleting Titles**
To delete chart or axis titles, select the title and press **Delete**.

✓ **Changing Title Display**
To switch the direction of the axis title, see Task 10.

1. To edit title text, click a chart or axis title twice (two single clicks, not a double-click).

2. With the flashing cursor inside the title text box, make the editing changes. Click anywhere outside the title to save the changes.

3. To format the title fonts, double-click a chart or axis title to display the Format dialog box.

4. On the Font tab of the Format dialog box, select a different font type, style, size, and color; then click **OK**. The new format is applied to the title.

Task 10: Changing Axis Title Orientation

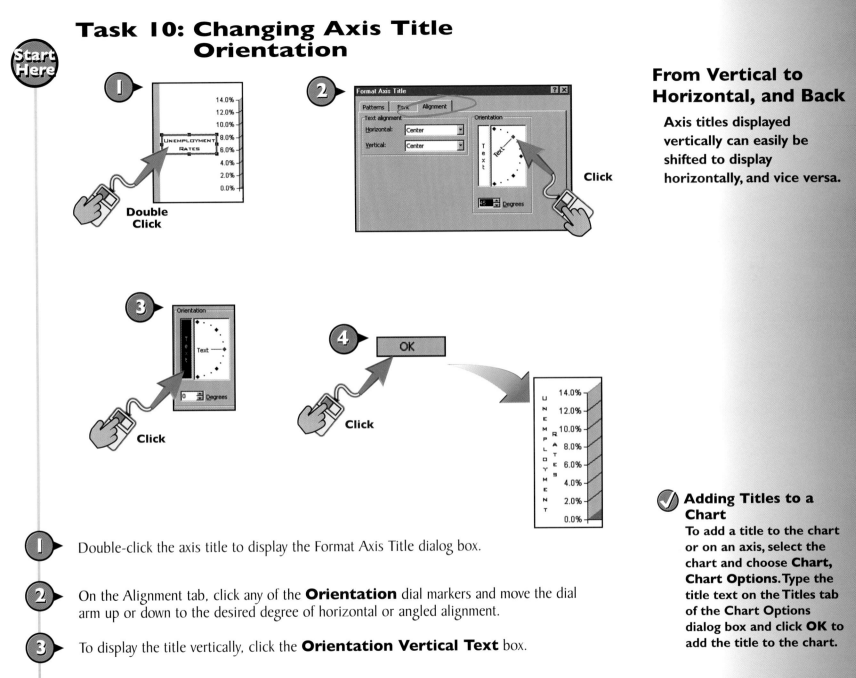

From Vertical to Horizontal, and Back

Axis titles displayed vertically can easily be shifted to display horizontally, and vice versa.

① Double-click the axis title to display the Format Axis Title dialog box.

② On the Alignment tab, click any of the **Orientation** dial markers and move the dial arm up or down to the desired degree of horizontal or angled alignment.

③ To display the title vertically, click the **Orientation Vertical Text** box.

④ Click **OK** to apply the changes to the axis title.

✓ Adding Titles to a Chart
To add a title to the chart or on an axis, select the chart and choose **Chart, Chart Options**. Type the title text on the **Titles** tab of the **Chart Options** dialog box and click **OK** to add the title to the chart.

Task 11: Formatting Chart Legends

Explaining Charts Better

The best charts are self-explanatory, presenting the underlying data clearly and completely. The chart legend, which identifies the series being plotted, is the key to the chart's information and an essential component of a clear chart.

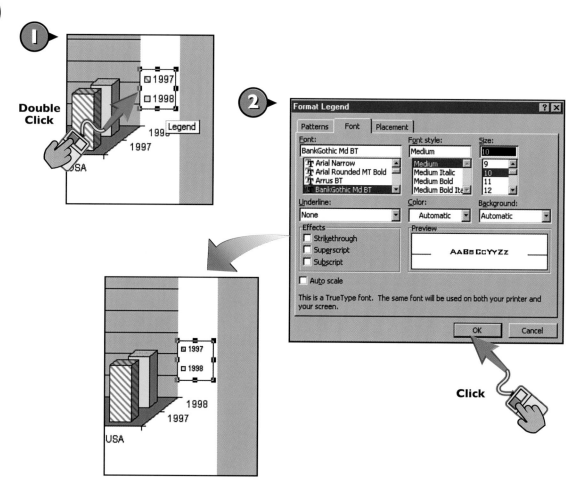

Double Click

Click

✓ **Moving or Deleting the Legend**
To move a legend, click it, hold down the left mouse button, and drag to a new location. To delete a legend, click it and press **Delete**.

✓ **Resizing the Legend**
To resize a legend, click it. Point at a selection handle, hold down the left mouse button, and drag to resize.

1. Double-click the chart legend to display the Format Legend dialog box.

2. Select a different font type, style, size, and color; then click **OK**. The changes are applied to the legend.

End Task

Task 12: Changing Chart Axes

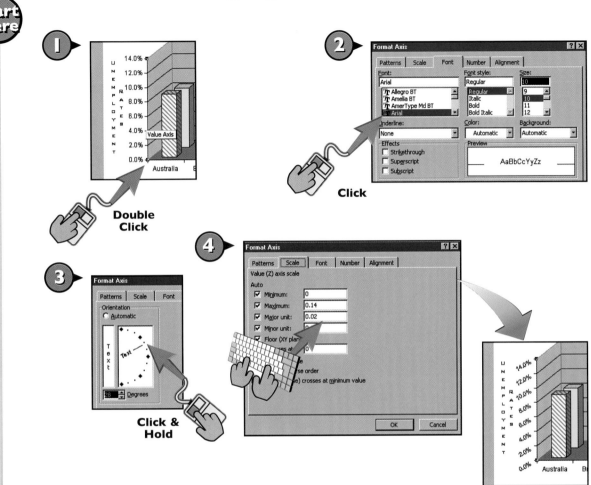

Click

Double Click

Click & Hold

Axis Adjustments

Chart axes are marked off in labeled *tick marks*, thin horizontal lines that indicate value or category changes. The labels, and even the scale of the axis, can be adjusted as needed.

✔ Changing the Axis Scale
For column, bar, cone, or cylinder charts whose data points look too similar to convey much information because their underlying values are close in size, adjust the Values axis scale on the Scale tab of the Format Axis dialog box. Minimum and Maximum values closer in size yield more sharply distinguished data points.

✔ Displaying Zero Values
If your chart data includes a zero value, resulting in a missing data point in the chart, double-click the Values axis and choose the **Scale** tab in the Format axis dialog box. Enter a non-zero value in the **Category Axis Crosses At** text box.

1 ▶ Double-click the axis to display the Format Axis dialog box.

2 ▶ To format the font of the axis labels, select the **Font** options on the Font tab of the Format Axis dialog box.

3 ▶ To change the orientation of the axis labels, click the desired degree of horizontal or angled alignment on the Alignment tab of the Format Axis dialog box.

4 ▶ To change the numerical increments used on the Value axis, type new values for the Minimum, Maximum, or Major Units on the Scale tab of the Format Axis dialog box.

End Task

Labels and Tables Clarify Charts

Data labels place the value of each data point on the chart next to the data point. Labeling data points makes charts more informative and less ambiguous. A data table is a grid beneath the chart, which displays each data point value and identifies each data series.

✓ **Editing Data Labels**
To change the data inside a data label, click the label twice (two single clicks, not a double-click) and type the new data.

✓ **Formatting Data Labels**
If your data labels are hard to read, try adjusting the font size and changing the font color. Double-click a data label to display the Format Data Label dialog box.

Task 13: Adding Data Labels and Data Tables to Charts

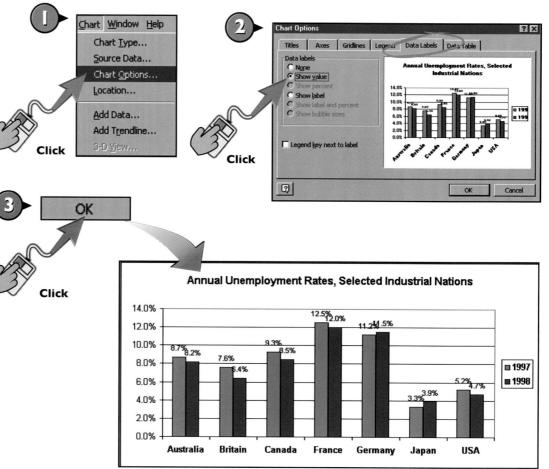

To add data labels to a chart, choose **Chart, Chart Options**. The Chart Options dialog box appears.

On the Data Labels tab, choose either **Show Value** (the value of each data point) or **Show Label** (the category label of each data point).

Click **OK** and a data label is placed next to each data point.

Next Step

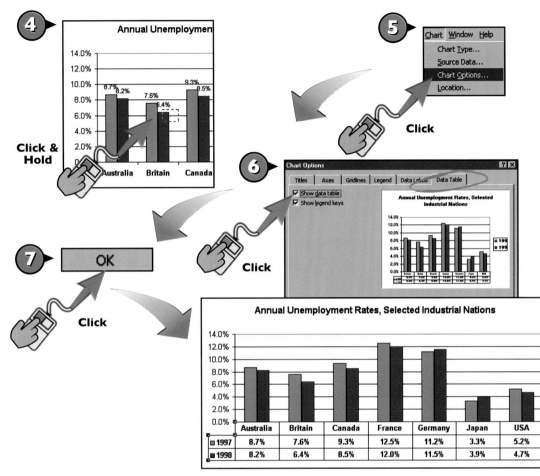

Annual Unemploymen

Click & Hold

Australia   Britain   Canada

Chart Window Help
Chart Type...
Source Data...
Chart Options...
Location...

Click

Chart Options

Titles | Axes | Gridlines | Legend | Data Labels | Data Table

☑ Show data table
☑ Show legend keys

Annual Unemployment Rates, Selected Industrial Nations

Click

OK

Click

Annual Unemployment Rates, Selected Industrial Nations

	Australia	Britain	Canada	France	Germany	Japan	USA
▣ 1997	8.7%	7.6%	9.3%	12.5%	11.2%	3.3%	5.2%
▪ 1998	8.2%	6.4%	8.5%	12.0%	11.5%	3.9%	4.7%

4️⃣ To change the placement of the labels, click once to select the series. Then hold down the left mouse button as you drag a label to a new location.

5️⃣ To add a data table to a chart, choose **Chart, Chart Options**. The Chart Options dialog box appears.

6️⃣ On the Data Table tab of the Chart Options dialog box, click **Show Data Table**.

7️⃣ Click **OK**. The chart displays with the data table attached below the category axis.

✅ **Legend Unnecessary with a data table**
When you add a data table to a chart, the legend is no longer needed. Select the legend and press **Delete** to remove it.

End Task

Task 14: Troubleshooting Pie and 3D Charts

Fixing 3D and Pie Charts

A very small slice in a pie chart can be hard to see. Likewise, many columns in a 3D column chart can obscure one another. Both problems are easily fixed.

✓ **Splitting the Pie**
To break a pie chart open, click once on the pie; a selection handle appears on the edge of each slice of pie. Drag any one of the pie slices away from center of the pie.

✓ **Avoid Obscuring Data**
Three-dimensional column, bar, cone, or pyramid charts containing many data series are difficult to read if some series obscure others. Consider changing to a two-dimensional chart type instead. See Task 3 to learn how to change the chart type.

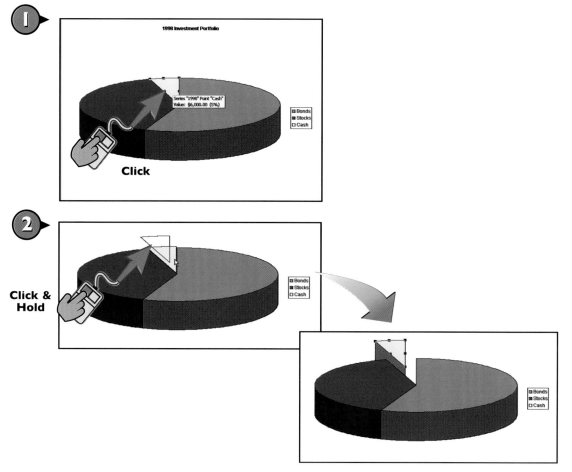

To "explode" a piece of pie—to pull one slice of pie away from the other slices—click twice (two single clicks, not a double-click) on the slice of the pie chart you want to explode.

Position the mouse pointer in the middle of the slice of pie, hold down the left mouse button, and drag the slice. The slice moves when you release the mouse button.

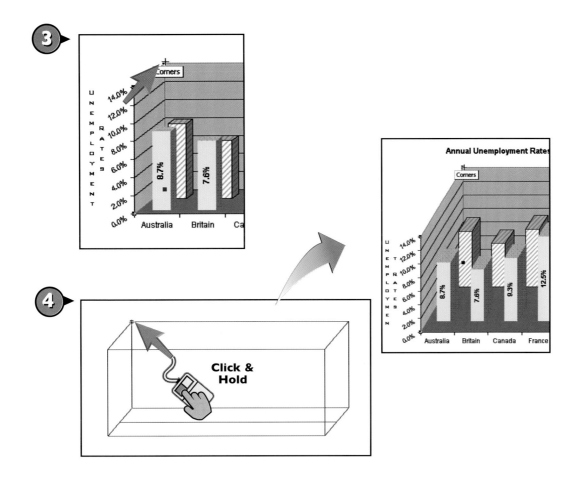

3 ► To adjust a 3D chart in which some of the data points are obscured, click any corner of the chart plot area.

4 ► Hold down the left mouse button and drag a chart corner. A "wire frame" appears to represent the plot area. Release the mouse button to adjust the chart orientation.

No Pie Slices?
If your pie chart appears with no slices, choose **Chart, Source Data.** Check to see if the data series are being plotted by rows or by columns. Changing the selection might add slices to your pie.

Creating a Compound Document

Charts illuminate numbers and dress up text reports. Incorporating an Excel chart into a Word document is largely a matter of copy and paste, with a few adjustments thrown in.

✓ **Quickly Switching Between Programs**
To switch between active program windows, press **Alt+Tab**. Hold down Alt and press Tab repeatedly to cycle through the open windows.

✓ **Linking to Create Automatic Updates**
For an Excel chart in a Word document that updates automatically whenever you update the Excel original, follow steps 1–4 of this Task. Then click **Edit, Paste Special**. In the Paste Special dialog box, click **Paste link** and click **OK**. Follow steps 6–8 to complete the operation.

Task 15: Adding an Excel Chart to a Word Document

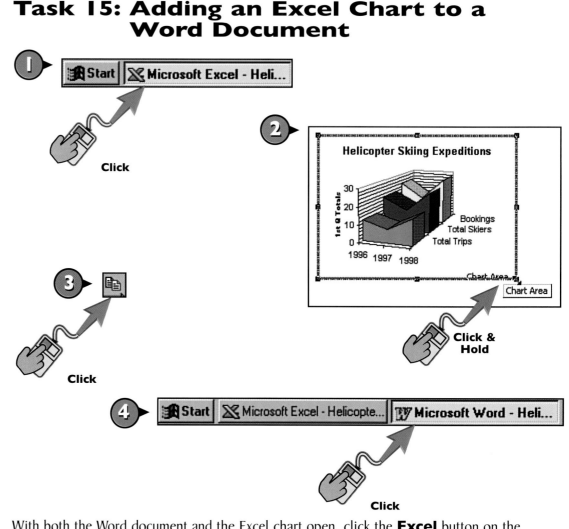

Helicopter Skiing Expeditions

Click

Click & Hold

Click

Click

1 With both the Word document and the Excel chart open, click the **Excel** button on the taskbar to switch to **Excel**.

2 Drag a corner of the Excel chart to resize it to its smallest readable size. See Tasks 4 and 5 for information about resizing embedded and chart sheet charts.

3 With the chart still selected, click the **Copy** button on Excel's Standard toolbar.

4 Click the **Word** button on the taskbar to switch to **Word**.

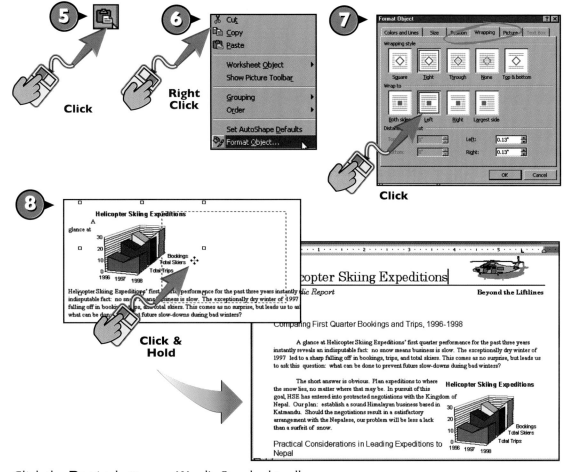

Click

Right Click

Click

Click & Hold

Helicopter Skiing Expeditions

A glance at Helicopter Skiing Expeditions' first quarter performance for the past three years instantly reveals an indisputable fact: no snow means business is slow. The exceptionally dry winter of 1997 led to a sharp falling off in bookings, trips, and total skiers. This comes as no surprise, but leads us to ask this question: what can be done to prevent future slow-downs during bad winters?

The short answer is obvious. Plan expeditions to where the snow lies, no matter where that may be. In pursuit of this goal, HSE has entered into protracted negotiations with the Kingdom of Nepal. Our plan: establish a sound Himalayan business based in Katmandu. Should the negotiations result in a satisfactory arrangement with the Nepalese, our problem will be less a lack than a surfeit of snow.

Practical Considerations in Leading Expeditions to Nepal

5 ► Click the **Paste** button on Word's Standard toolbar.

6 ► To format the chart in Word, right-click the pasted chart in Word and choose **Format Object** from the shortcut menu.

7 ► On the Wrapping tab of the Format Object dialog box, choose a **Wrapping Style** and one of the positions the chart should **Wrap To**. Then click **OK**.

8 ► Drag the chart to the desired location in the document.

Resizing in Excel Is Easier
Although you can resize charts in Word, making all your sizing adjustments in Excel first, before copying the chart to Word, is easier.

WARNING
Always save your work before copying and pasting between Microsoft Office programs. The likelihood of the Office programs crashing increases greatly when you transfer material between them.

Working with Graphics

Numbers might be exciting to accountants, but for most of us, columns and rows of data lack visual impact. That doesn't mean worksheets have to be dull. Excel is packed with tools to add pictures and other worksheet-enlivening graphic touches.

Part 9 explores the use of two graphics features for enlivening any worksheet significantly—clip art and WordArt. You will learn to insert and modify the clip art that comes with Microsoft Office. Additionally, you will see how to create high-impact titles with WordArt.

Tasks

Task 1: Inserting Clip Art

Adding Graphics to Worksheets

Your copy of Excel comes with an extensive collection of clip art, pictures, and other graphics that are ready to be inserted into worksheets.

Included in the Clip Gallery are business clips, currency clips, flags, and industrial clips.

✓ More Clips on the Office CD

Depending on how Excel was installed on your computer, all the available categories of clips might not appear when you access the Clip Gallery. Insert the Microsoft Office 97 CD and access the Clip Gallery. The categories should reflect what is on your PC as well as what is on the CD.

✓ Clip Descriptions

When you select a clip from the Gallery, a description of the clip appears at the bottom of the dialog box.

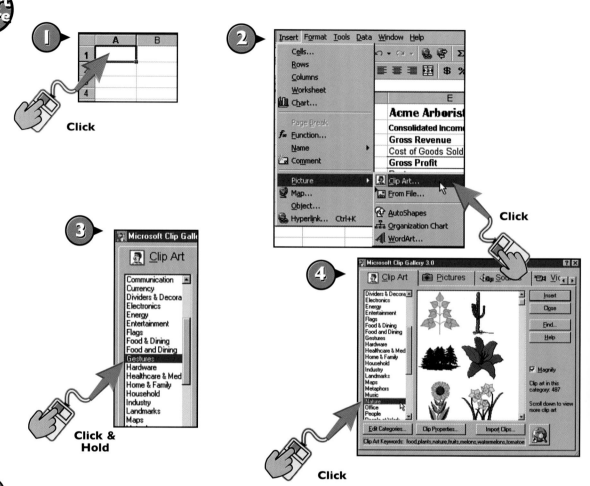

1. To insert a clip art image, select the cell you want to be at the upper-left corner of the image.

2. Choose **Insert, Picture, Clip Art**.

3. In the Microsoft Clip Gallery 3.0 dialog box, scroll down in the left pane to see the list of categories.

4. Click the desired category.

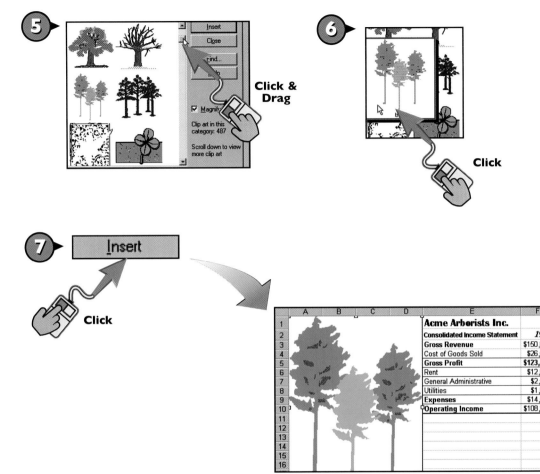

**Click &
Drag**

Click

Click

WARNING
If you get an error message
when trying to insert clip
art, place your Microsoft
Office 97 CD into the
computer's CD-ROM drive
and try again.

**Moving and Resizing
Clip Art**
Moving clip art around the
worksheet is easy, so where
the image is first inserted
isn't important. See Task 2
for more information on
moving and resizing clips.

Clips on the Web
If you can't find the image
you are looking for in the
Clip Gallery 3.0 dialog box,
see Part 11, Task 5, for
information on accessing
more clip art images.

5 In the right pane of the Microsoft Clip Gallery 3.0 dialog box, scroll through the available
pictures in the selected category.

6 Click to select the clip art image you want to insert into your worksheet.

7 Click **Insert** in the Microsoft Clip Gallery 3.0 dialog box. The selected image is inserted
into the worksheet and the Microsoft Clip Gallery 3.0 closes.

End
Task

Task 2: Moving and Resizing Clip Art

Fitting Clip Art to the Worksheet

After you insert clip art on your worksheet, simple drag-and-drop maneuvers can tailor its size and location.

Start Here

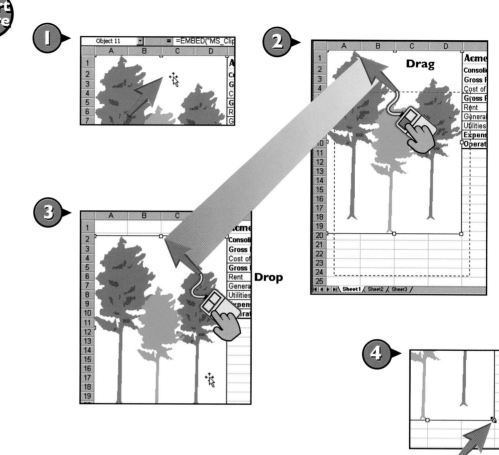

Drag

Drop

Selection Handles
If you click outside the inserted clip art image, the image loses its selection handles, which are necessary for resizing the clip art. Click the image again to regain the selection handles.

Picture Toolbar
The Picture toolbar pops up automatically when you insert clip art. If the toolbar gets in your way, drag it by its title bar. See Task 4 for information on using the Picture toolbar.

To move an inserted clip art image around the worksheet, move the pointer inside the image. The pointer becomes a combination white arrow and four-headed black arrow.

Hold down the left mouse button and drag the image. A dotted border moves with the pointer, indicating where the image will be placed.

Release the mouse button to place the image in the new location.

To resize a clip art image, point at any of the four corner selection handles. The pointer becomes a double-headed arrow.

Next Step

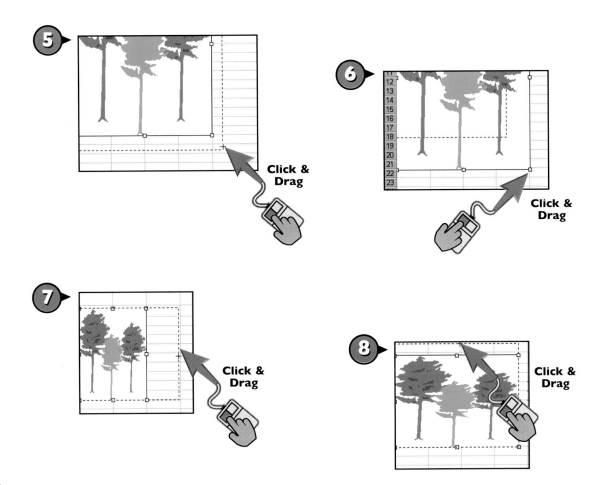

5 Hold down the left mouse button and drag a corner selection handle outward to expand the image.

6 Hold down the left mouse button and drag a corner selection handle inward to shrink the image.

7 For a longer, flatter image, drag one of the side selection handles.

8 For a taller, narrower image, drag a top or bottom selection handle.

✔ **Keyboard Method Provides Control**
For precision clip art moves, click the image to select it. Then use the arrow keys to move the image to the new location.

Page
157

Task 3: Changing Clip Art Colors

Customizing Clip Art

Clip art objects look like finished products, but they can be altered in many ways. The quickest change is a new color scheme.

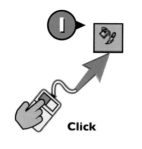

Click

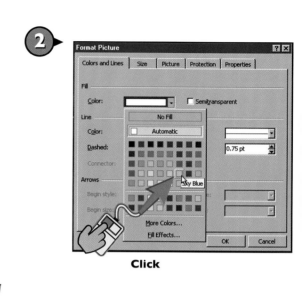

Click

OK

Click

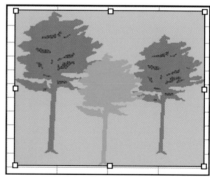

✓ **Remove the Clip Border**
To eliminate the box around an inserted image, click the **Line Color** drop-down arrow on the Colors and Lines tab of the Format Picture dialog box. Then choose **No Line** from the Line Color menu.

✓ **Displaying the Picture Toolbar**
If you don't see the Picture toolbar, right-click the image and choose **Show Picture Toolbar**.

1 After you select the clip art image, click the **Format Picture** button on the Picture toolbar to display the Format Picture dialog box.

2 On the Colors and Lines tab of the Format Picture dialog box, click the **Fill Color** drop-down arrow and choose a new color from the color menu.

3 Click **OK** in the Format Picture dialog box. The color change is applied to the image.

Task 4: Modifying Clip Art Objects

Start Here

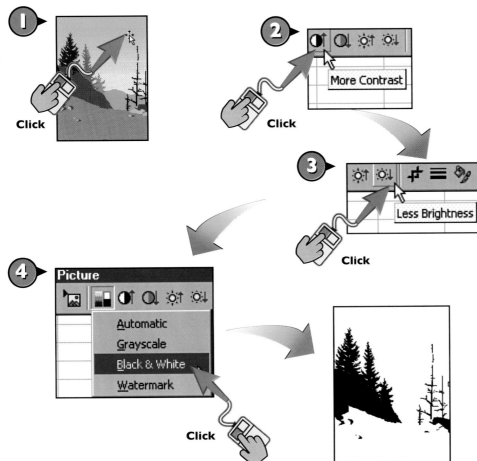

1 Click

2 More Contrast · Click

3 Less Brightness · Click

4 Picture
Automatic
Grayscale
Black & White
Watermark
Click

More Picture Customizing

If you need a brighter or darker picture, or a black-and-white image instead of color, the **Picture** toolbar has the necessary controls to modify the clip art image.

---

1 Click to select the clip art image. The Picture toolbar appears.

2 To modify the image contrast, click the **More Contrast** or **Less Contrast** button on the Picture toolbar.

3 To modify the image brightness, click the **More Brightness** or **Less Brightness** button on the Picture toolbar.

4 To create a simplified black-and-white image, click the **Image Control** button on the Picture toolbar and select **Black & White**.

✅ **Creating Watermarks**
For a fainter image, suitable for a worksheet background, click the **Image Control** button on the Picture toolbar and choose **Watermark**.

End Task

Page
159

Task 5: Creating WordArt Titles

Art with Text

Dramatic worksheet titles and banners are easy to create with Excel's WordArt feature. WordArt takes ordinary text, enhances it through color, and displays it in interesting arcs, curves, and angles.

✓ WordArt's Yellow Diamond

To skew the angle of the object, drag the yellow diamond displayed with a selected WordArt object.

✓ Moving and Resizing WordArt

Like a clip art object, WordArt can be resized, moved, and otherwise modified. See Task 8 for more information.

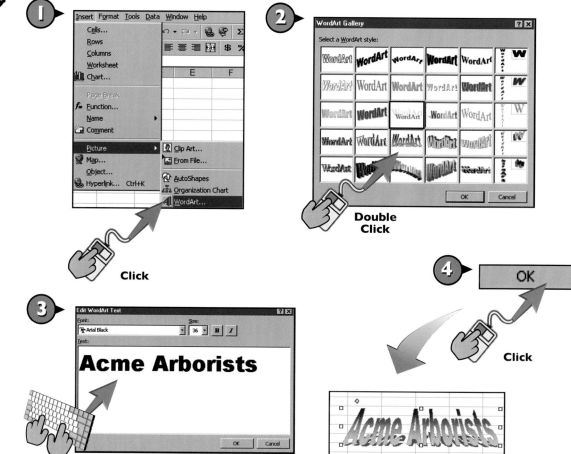

 To create a WordArt object, click **Insert, Picture, WordArt**.

 In the WordArt Gallery, double-click any of the WordArt styles.

3 In the Edit WordArt Text dialog box, type your title.

4 Click **OK** in the Edit WordArt dialog box. The WordArt object is inserted in the worksheet, and the WordArt toolbar is displayed.

Next Step

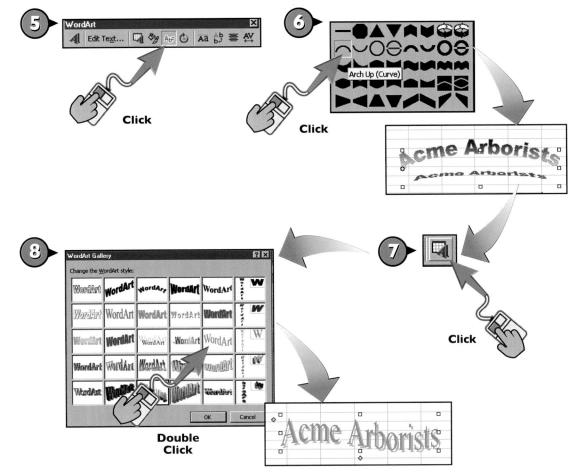

5 To change the WordArt object's shape, click the **WordArt Shape** button on the WordArt toolbar.

6 Click a shape on the menu that appears; the WordArt object assumes the new shape.

7 Click the **WordArt Gallery** button on the WordArt toolbar.

8 Double-click another style; the text is displayed, using the new style.

Click

Click

Click

Double
Click

✓ **Rotating WordArt Objects**
From the WordArt toolbar, click the **Free Rotate** button. Position the mouse pointer over any of the green rotation handles at the four corners of the WordArt Object. Hold down the left mouse button and drag the pointer to rotate the object. Press **Esc** to get rid of the rotation handles.

✓ **Recoloring WordArt Objects**
To change WordArt colors, click the **Format WordArt** button on the WordArt toolbar. Click the **Colors and Lines** tab in the Format WordArt dialog box, choose a color from the Fill Color drop-down menu, and click **OK** to apply the change.

End
Task

Using 3D for Extra Special Effects

Three-dimensional options can jazz up WordArt objects for truly startling results. The Drawing toolbar is only the starting point for applying 3D options; the 3D Settings toolbar provides additional options.

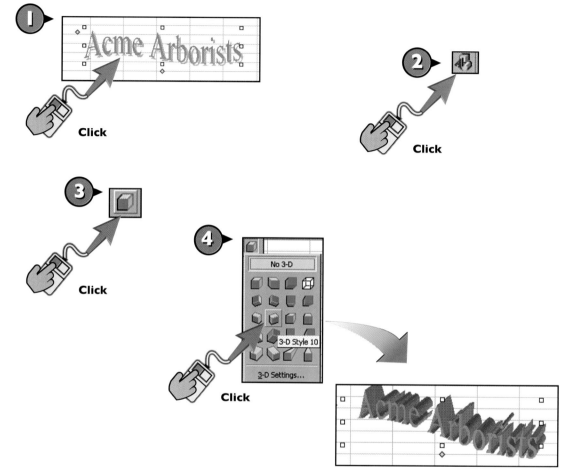

✓ **Adding Texture to WordArt Objects**
Click the **Surface** button on the 3D Settings toolbar and choose a different texture for your 3D effect.

✓ **Explore the 3D Settings Toolbar**
The many variations in size, depth, and color offered by the 3D Settings toolbar are too numerous to mention individually. Experiment with the effects until you get the results you want.

1 ▶ Click to select the WordArt object.

2 ▶ Click the **Drawing** button on the Standard toolbar to display the Drawing toolbar.

3 ▶ Click the **3D** button on the Drawing toolbar.

4 ▶ Click any of the styles on the 3D menu. The selected style is applied to the WordArt object.

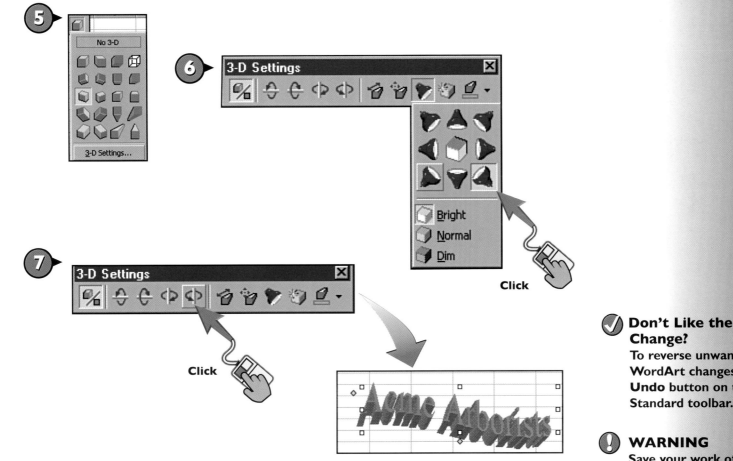

Click

Click

Don't Like the Change?
To reverse unwanted WordArt changes, click the **Undo** button on the Standard toolbar.

⚠️ **WARNING**
Save your work often as you experiment with different WordArt effects. These graphics features place a greater than normal strain on your computer's resources and can lead to a system freeze-up.

5 ▶ To modify the 3D effect, click the 3D button on the Drawing toolbar and choose **3D Settings** to display the 3D Settings toolbar.

6 ▶ Click the **Lighting** button on the 3D Settings toolbar and choose a different lighting angle (the angle from which the 3D object appears to be illuminated).

7 ▶ Click any of the four **Tilt** buttons on the 3D Settings toolbar to adjust the angle at which the WordArt object is displayed.

Task 7: Changing WordArt Fonts

Customizing WordArt

Different font types and font sizes modify WordArt in effective ways. Use the Edit Text button on the WordArt toolbar to change the WordArt font options.

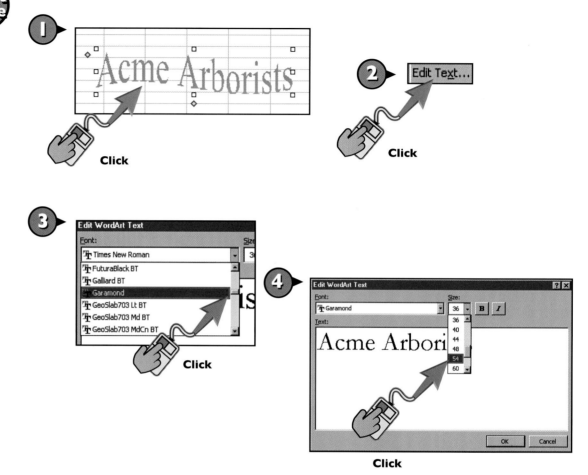

Click

Click

Click

Click

✓ **Displaying Text Vertically**
To stack WordArt text vertically, click the **WordArt Vertical Text** button on the WordArt toolbar.

✓ **WordArt Styles Impact Font Options**
The Bold and Italic buttons in the Edit WordArt Text might not have the expected effect on WordArt objects, depending on the WordArt style in use.

 Click the WordArt object to select it; the WordArt toolbar appears.

 Click the **Edit Text** button on the WordArt toolbar to display the Edit WordArt Text dialog box.

Click the **Size** drop-down arrow and select a different font size if desired; then click **OK** to apply the changes.

In the Edit WordArt Text dialog box, click the **Font** drop-down arrow and choose a different font.

Task 8: Moving and Resizing WordArt

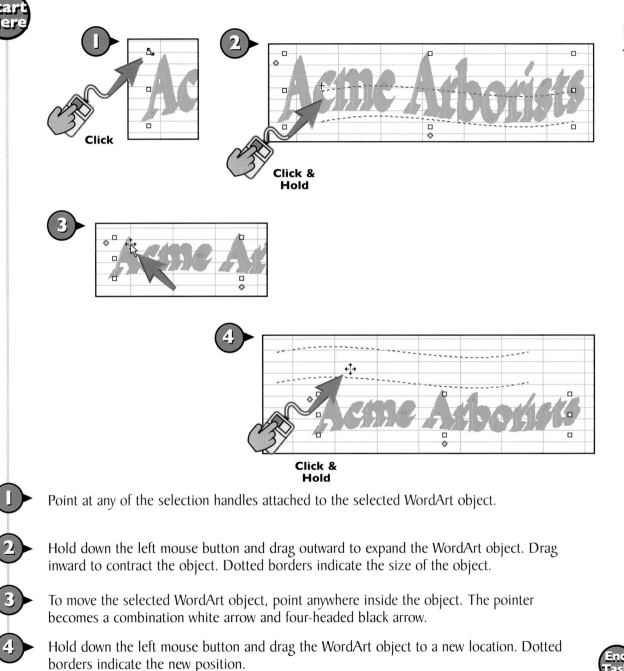

Click

Click & Hold

Click & Hold

Fitting WordArt to the Worksheet

Like clip art and other inserted objects, WordArt is easily moved and resized with a few simple steps.

 Keep the WordArt Proportional
Drag a corner selection handle to expand or contract a WordArt object with its original proportions.

 Deleting WordArt Objects
To delete any inserted object, click to select the object and then press **Delete**.

1. Point at any of the selection handles attached to the selected WordArt object.

2. Hold down the left mouse button and drag outward to expand the WordArt object. Drag inward to contract the object. Dotted borders indicate the size of the object.

3. To move the selected WordArt object, point anywhere inside the object. The pointer becomes a combination white arrow and four-headed black arrow.

4. Hold down the left mouse button and drag the WordArt object to a new location. Dotted borders indicate the new position.

End Task

Working with Lists

An Excel list is a database of information, generally relating to one particular topic. Any kind of data is suitable for a list, from a catalog of old LPs to a phone book of names and addresses or a list of products you sell. Creating a list in Excel enables you to store and maintain your data with ease and opens up a large number of Excel features you can use to manipulate the data, all described in Part 10.

Lists are sortable alphabetically, numerically, or by any other relevant criteria. You can create subtotals and grand totals from a list. Lists are also searchable. Filters enable you to extract from a list only the information you need for printing reports and for simply viewing the trees in a forest of data.

Tasks

Task 1: Creating a List

Instant Databases

A few simple guidelines distinguish lists from other kinds of worksheets. Follow them, and you'll have an instant database.

Excel lists must use the first row for labeling each column of information.

There can be no blank rows or columns within the list.

Start Here

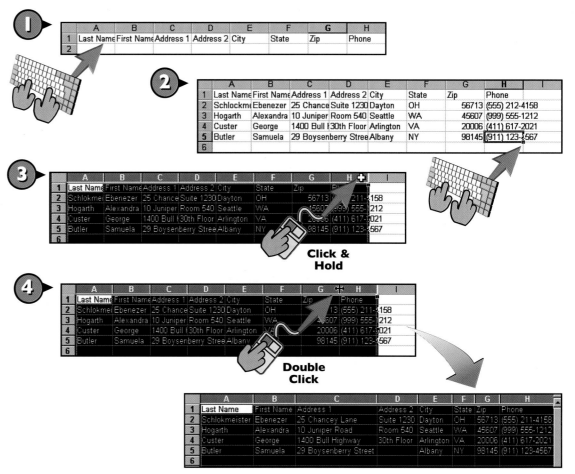

Click & Hold

Double Click

✓ **Formatting Excel Lists**
To help distinguish one row in the list from another, use one of the List formats in the AutoFormat feature (see Part 5, Task 18).

1 Select the cell that will contain the heading for your first column of data. Type the column headings, pressing **Tab** after each entry (for example, **Last Name**, **First Name**, and so on).

2 In the row immediately below the row of headings, start typing the information you want to maintain in the list. Don't leave any blank rows within the list.

3 If necessary, widen the columns so all data can be viewed. To widen multiple columns at the same time, first highlight the worksheet column headings.

4 Position the mouse pointer on the right border of any highlighted worksheet column and double-click. The columns are fitted to the widest data.

End Task

Task 2: Adding Data to a List with the Data Form

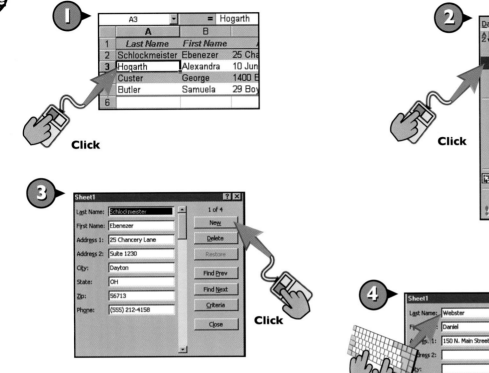

Click

Click

Click

Click

Excel's Handy Data Form

Data entry is tedious at best, but Excel's Data Form makes the chore a little easier. Based on the column headings in your list, Excel creates a form to use for adding data. New data is always added to the bottom of the list.

✓ **List Terminology**
In a list, each row of information is called a record. Each labeled column of information within a record is called a field. Each field entered in the data form is placed in columns of the list.

⓵ **WARNING**
Don't click the **Restore** button in the Data Form. Clicking **Restore** erases any data you've typed for a new entry.

---

1 Click any cell in your list.

2 Choose **Data, Form**. The Data Form appears, with your column labels as data entry fields.

3 Click **New** in the Data Form.

4 Type a new entry. Repeat steps 3 and 4 for any additional entries, and click **Close** to add the data to your list.

End Task

Task 3: Finding List Records

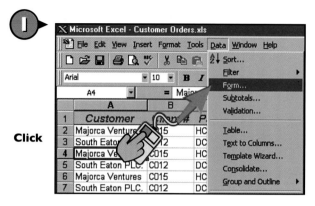

Fast List Searches

As lists begin to grow, tracking down a specific record is made easier with the help of the Data Form. You enter an example of the data you are looking for, and the Data Form locates all records that meet your criteria.

Click

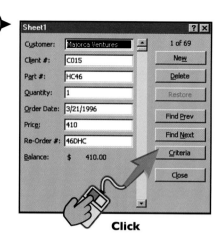

Click

Click

Click

 **A Searching Alternative**

You can also use the Find feature in Excel to locate information. Choose **Edit, Find** and type part of a record in the Find dialog box; then press **Find Next**.

 Sorting Improves Searching

Sorting lists makes records easier to find. See Task 5 for more information on sorting your list.

1 ▸ Click any cell in the list and then choose **Data, Form**.

2 ▸ In the Data Form, click **Criteria** to clear the Data Form fields.

3 ▸ Click one of the field edit boxes and type the data you are looking for. The form is not case sensitive, and you can type partial entries (for example, to find Saltaire Inc, type **salt**).

4 ▸ Click **Find Next** and the first record matching your criteria appears in the Data Form. Click **Find Next** again to see the next record matching the criteria.

Task 4: Editing List Records

Start Here

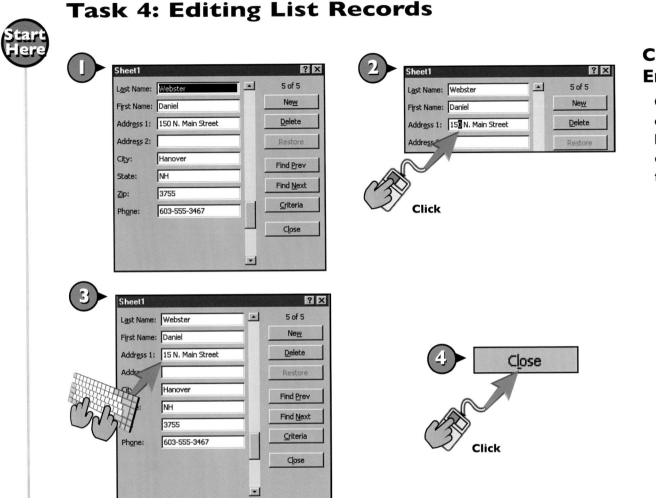

Correcting Data Entry Errors

Correcting typing mistakes or updating records is just like editing any other type of data in Excel. First you find it, and then you fix it.

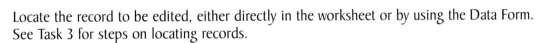

1 ▶ Locate the record to be edited, either directly in the worksheet or by using the Data Form. See Task 3 for steps on locating records.

2 ▶ Click the field in the Data Form or the cell in the worksheet to be corrected or updated.

3 ▶ Type the correction.

4 ▶ Click **Close** in the Data Form or press **Enter** while in the worksheet to accept the changes.

✔ **Same Change to Multiple Records**
For making a global update—the same change to many records—choose **Edit, Replace.** See Part 3, Task 14, for more information.

End Task

Task 5: Sorting Lists

The A to Z of Lists

Sorting is rearranging a list to make it easier to use or to reveal information about the data. Lists can be sorted in ascending or descending order, alphabetically, numerically, or by other criteria.

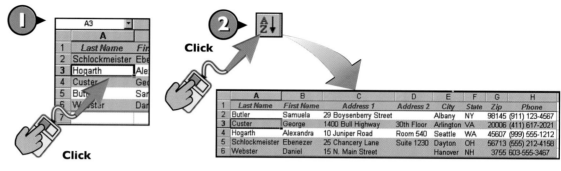

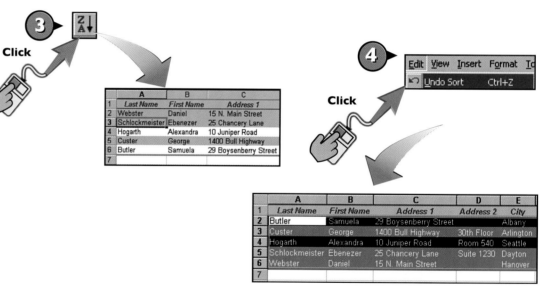

WARNING

To sort your entire list, click just one cell (any cell) in the list. If you select multiple cells, such as a column, Excel sorts just the data that is highlighted.

Multiple Column Sorts

For more elaborate sorts by multiple criteria, choose **Data, Sort,** and fill in the Sort By and Then By text boxes. For example, sort first by the State column and then by the City column.

1 ▶ Click a cell in the column by which you want to sort the list. To sort by Last Name, for example, click any cell in the **Last Name** column. Do not click the worksheet column heading.

2 ▶ Click the **Sort Ascending** button on the Standard toolbar to sort the list in order from lowest to highest (for example, A–Z or 0–9).

3 ▶ Click the **Sort Descending** button to sort the list from highest to lowest (for example, Z–A or 9–0).

4 ▶ To restore the list to the order it was in before you sorted, choose **Edit, Undo Sort**. To restore lists that have been sorted many times, see Task 6.

Task 6: Undoing Sorts

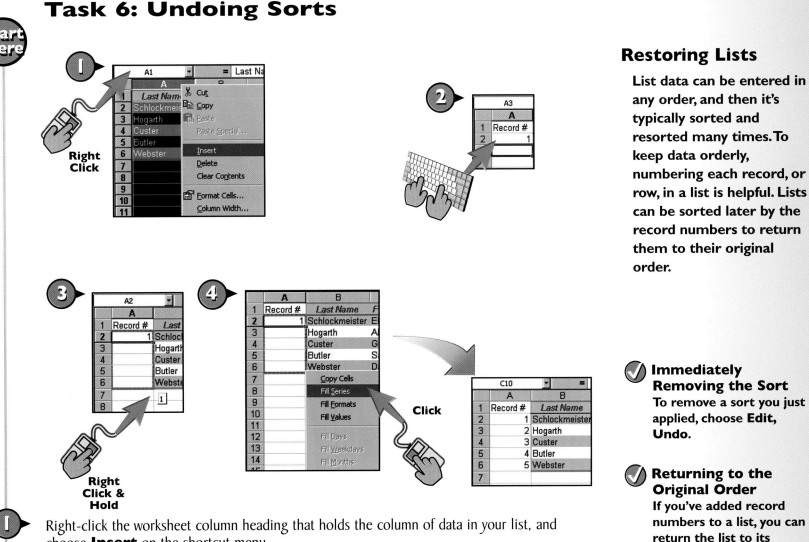

Restoring Lists

List data can be entered in any order, and then it's typically sorted and resorted many times. To keep data orderly, numbering each record, or row, in a list is helpful. Lists can be sorted later by the record numbers to return them to their original order.

✓ **Immediately Removing the Sort**
To remove a sort you just applied, choose **Edit, Undo**.

✓ **Returning to the Original Order**
If you've added record numbers to a list, you can return the list to its original order by selecting any cell in the record number column and clicking the **Sort Ascending** button on the Standard toolbar.

---

1 ▶ Right-click the worksheet column heading that holds the column of data in your list, and choose **Insert** on the shortcut menu.

2 ▶ In the new column, select the column heading. Type **Record #** for the column heading and press **Enter**. Type **1** in the next cell and press **Enter**.

3 ▶ Click again in the cell containing the number 1. Point at the fill handle in the lower-right corner of the cell. Press the right mouse button and drag down the column to the bottom.

4 ▶ Choose **Fill Series** on the shortcut menu. Every record is now numbered, starting with number 1.

Task 7: Extracting List Data with AutoFilter

Start Here

Filtering Data for Clarity's Sake

Data filters work like coffee filters; they take out what you don't want and leave what you do. Hiding unnecessary detail in a big list lets you make better sense of the data by displaying only what you want to see. A filtered list can be printed, just as you would print any worksheet.

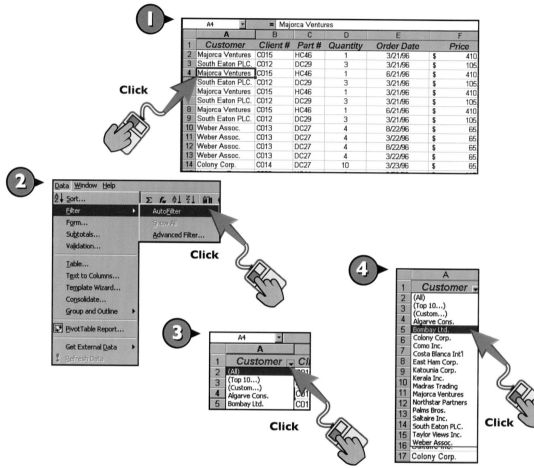

Click

Click

Click

Click

✓ **Applying Multiple Filters**

To further filter your data, choose a filter drop-down arrow in another column in your list and select the criteria.

1 ▶ Click any cell in the list.

2 ▶ Choose **Data, Filter, AutoFilter**. Drop-down arrows appear next to the column headings in your list.

3 ▶ Click the drop-down arrow in the column whose data you want to filter.

4 ▶ Choose one of the entries in the selected drop-down menu.

Next Step

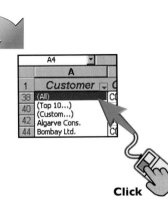

Click

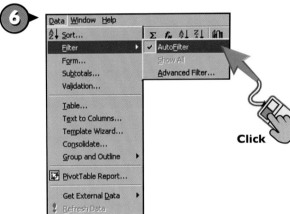

Click

The rest of the list is hidden. To see the whole list again, click the selected column's drop-down arrow and choose **(All)**. The filter is removed.

To remove the AutoFilter drop-down arrows, choose **Data, Filter, AutoFilter**.

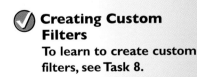
Top Ten AutoFilter
AutoFilter's Top Ten choice on the drop-down menu enables you to choose any number of records from either the top or the bottom of the list as your filtering criterion.

Creating Custom Filters
To learn to create custom filters, see Task 8.

Task 8: Customizing AutoFilter

Refining AutoFilter Criteria

The AutoFilter lets you see list detail, but you can only filter based on the specific entries in the column. Customize AutoFilter to broaden the filtering criteria. Instead of viewing data relevant to only one client, for example, you can view data pertaining to two different clients.

✓ Understanding "And" Criteria

Choosing **And** in the Custom AutoFilter dialog box displays only rows that satisfy both conditions in the Custom AutoFilter boxes.

✓ Why Use Custom Filters?

Custom filters are often used with numerical data to filter on a range of numbers. Examples include displaying customers who ordered more than five items or orders placed between the 1st and the 15th of the month.

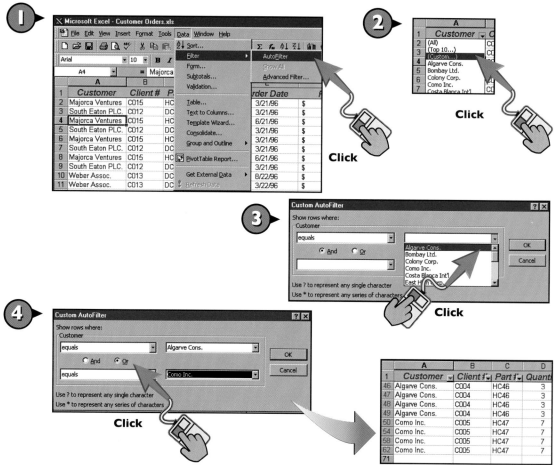

Click

Click

Click

Click

Click

1 ▶ Click any cell in your list. Then choose **Data, Filter, AutoFilter**.

2 ▶ Click the **AutoFilter** drop-down arrow in the column whose data you want to filter, and choose **(Custom)** on the drop-down menu.

3 ▶ In the Custom AutoFilter dialog box, click the drop-down arrow in the upper left box and choose a comparison operator. Click the box on the right and choose from the list of entries.

4 ▶ In the Custom AutoFilter dialog box, click the **Or** radio button and repeat step 3 to select additional criteria. Click **OK** to apply the custom filter.

Task 9: List-Formatting Tips

1

2

3

Click

Click

4

Do's and Don'ts of Lists

The challenge in formatting a list is to make row upon row of data readable. If you prefer to design your own list and skip the Excel AutoFormats, keep the following tips in mind.

1 ▶ Don't leave any blank rows or columns in a list. Excel treats a blank as the end of the list, so data below a blank row is not included in sorts or filters.

2 ▶ Distinguish the header row from the rest of the list. Select the header row and click the **Fill Color** drop-down arrow on the Formatting toolbar.

3 ▶ Choose a color as a background color behind the text. While the header row is selected, click the **Bold** and **Italic** buttons to set the header row off from the rest of the list.

4 ▶ Don't put two lists on the same worksheet. Printing, sorting, and filtering are more problematic if you do.

✓ Printing Formatted Lists

Printed lists have the same formatting as onscreen lists, so consider how the printout will look when you're choosing formatting.

Task 10: Producing List Subtotals

Extracting Useful Information from Lists

Subtotals take a portion of your list data and summarize it. On a list of customer purchases, for example, subtotals could show what each customer owes or what product each customer orders. Before you can produce subtotals, you must sort the list on the criteria you want to subtotal. To produce customer subtotals, for example, you would sort the list on the Customer field.

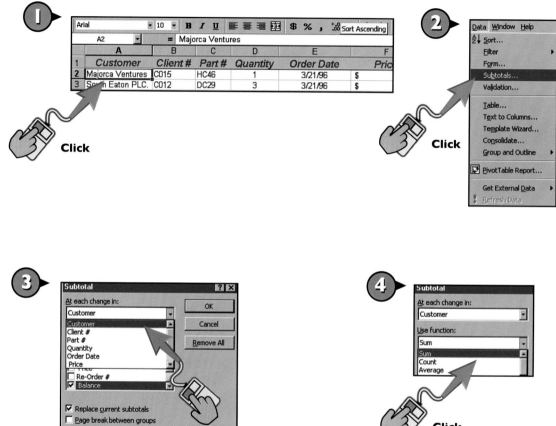

✅ **Printing Lists with Subtotals**

Subtotals print as they display, so to produce a subtotal report, subtotal the list and print it.

① Click a cell in the column whose data you want to subtotal; then click the **Sort Ascending** button on the Standard toolbar to sort the list.

② Choose **Data, Subtotals**.

③ In the Subtotal dialog box, click the **At Each Change In** drop-down menu and choose the same field on which you sorted the list.

④ From the Use Function drop-down menu, choose a calculation (for example, Sum) to appear below each group in the field to which you are applying the subtotal.

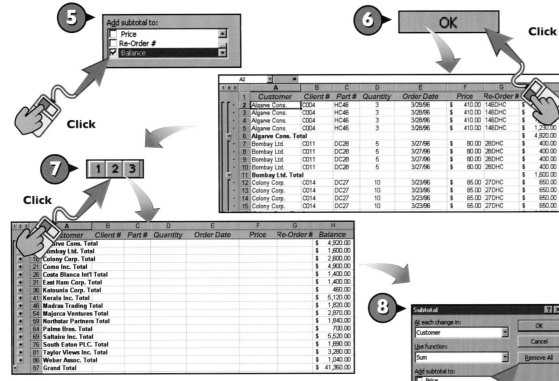

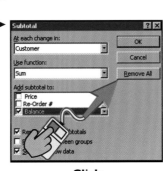

Click

✓ **Creating Charts from Subtotals**
Subtotaled lists make good charts. Select a subtotaled section of the list and click the **Chart Wizard** button on the Standard toolbar. However, if you remove or change a subtotal, the chart will change.

(5) In the Add Subtotal To box, choose the field to subtotal.

(6) Choose **OK** in the Subtotal dialog box to display the subtotals in the list.

✓ **Sort and Subtotal the Same Column**
The column selected in the **At Each Change In** box in the Subtotal dialog box should be the same column on which you sorted the list.

(7) Click the Outline numbers to the left of the subtotaled list to display or hide detail. For example, click **2** to view only the second level of list detail.

(8) To remove subtotals, choose **Data, Subtotals**. In the Subtotal dialog box, choose **Remove All** and then choose **OK**.

Working with the Internet

Even the smallest personal computer can store vast repositories of diverse information—your personal library. Any computer with an Internet connection becomes its own public library, with access to information stored on other computers worldwide.

In this part, you learn how to use Excel to access some of the resources on the Internet. From clip art to stock prices, Excel has tools to bring home useful data of all types.

You must have a Web browser such as Netscape Navigator or Microsoft Internet Explorer to perform the tasks in this part.

Tasks

Task 1: Browsing the Web from Excel

Start Here

Excel's Direct Internet Connection

Your Web browser is a single click away when you work in Excel. Whether you are tracking stock prices or planning a vacation, you needn't leave Excel.

✓ **Investor's Web Sites**
Useful Web sites for investors include `http://www.dbc.com`, the Data Broadcasting Corporation Site, packed with financial information and market news. The Microsoft Investor site at `http://investor.msn.com` is also a valuable investor resource.

✓ **Traveler's Web Sites**
Exceptionally good general interest Web sites include `http://www.mapquest.com`, a terrific online road atlas that can even provide door-to-door driving instructions. Entire vacations, real or armchair, can be planned through Microsoft's online travel agency at `http://expedia.msn.com`.

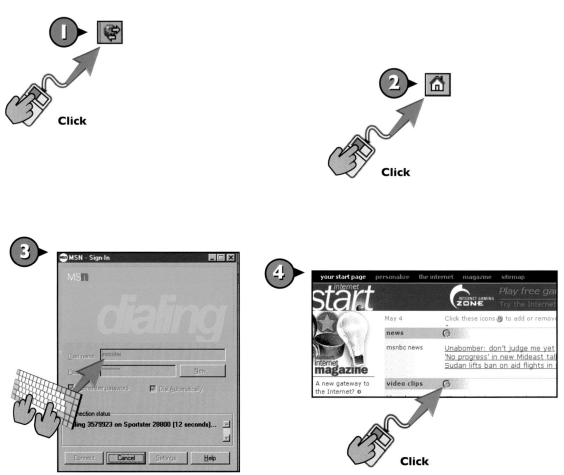

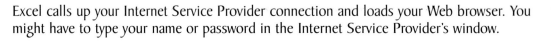

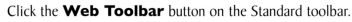
1 Click the **Web Toolbar** button on the Standard toolbar.

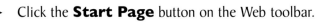
2 Click the **Start Page** button on the Web toolbar.

3 Excel calls up your Internet Service Provider connection and loads your Web browser. You might have to type your name or password in the Internet Service Provider's window.

4 After the Start Page loads, click any of the *links* to travel around the Web.

Next Step

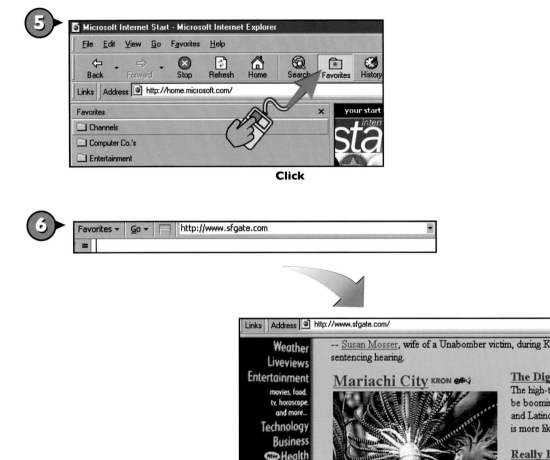

Click

5 ▶ Internet Explorer users can click the Favorites button on the browser's toolbar and choose a Web site from your list of favorite sites.

6 ▶ If you know the address of a Web site you'd like to see, type the site's address directly into the Address box on the Web toolbar in Excel and press **Enter**.

⚠ **WARNING**
The World Wide Web is still in its infancy. Moving around on the Web can be very slow, links don't always work, and software viruses abound. If you download files from Web sites you are not familiar with, save the downloads to disk and scan them with a virus-checking program before you open them. Among several good virus detector programs available are Norton's AntiVirus and McAfee's VirusScan.

✓ **Revisit Old Favorites**
When you come across a Web site you plan to revisit, you can add the site to a "shortcut" list for quick return access. In Netscape Navigator, the list is called Bookmarks; in Internet Explorer, it's called Favorites. To revisit a listed site, just display the list and click the site name.

Task 2: Importing Internet Data

Import Stock Quotes into your Worksheet

If you follow the stock market, Excel's stock quote import feature might be very useful for importing data directly into a worksheet for analysis and storage. Many other types of data imports are available as well.

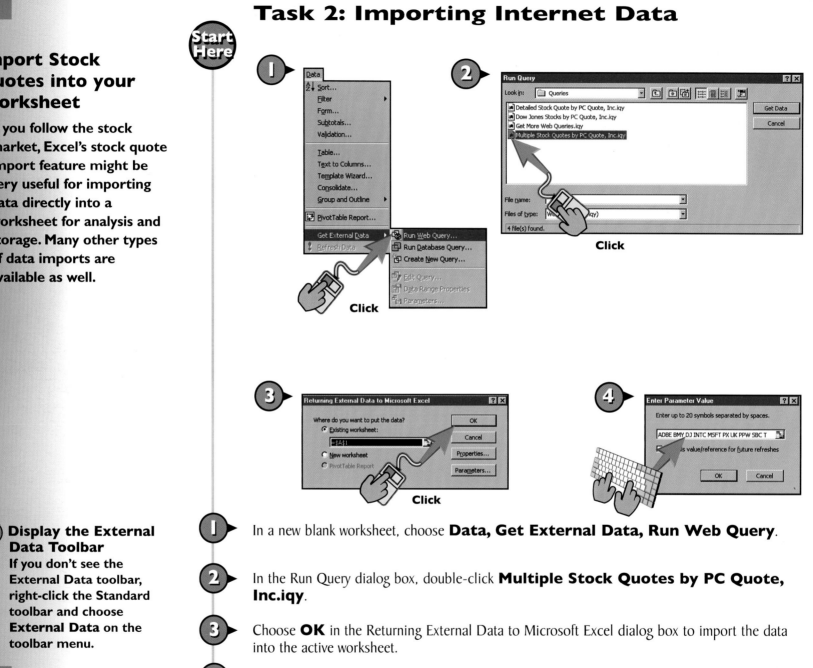

Start Here

Click

Click

Click

Click

(✓) **Display the External Data Toolbar**
If you don't see the External Data toolbar, right-click the Standard toolbar and choose **External Data** on the toolbar menu.

1 In a new blank worksheet, choose **Data, Get External Data, Run Web Query**.

2 In the Run Query dialog box, double-click **Multiple Stock Quotes by PC Quote, Inc.iqy**.

3 Choose **OK** in the Returning External Data to Microsoft Excel dialog box to import the data into the active worksheet.

4 In the Enter Parameter Value dialog box, type up to 20 stock ticker symbols, following each one by a space. Click **OK** to retrieve the data on the stocks you specified.

Next Step

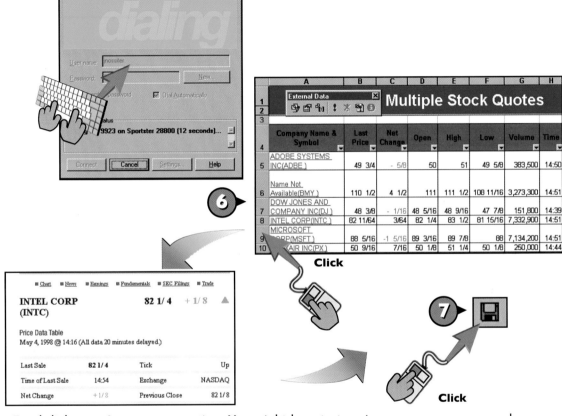

Click

Click

5 ▶ Excel dials your Internet connection. You might have to type in your name or password.

6 ▶ The stocks represented by the symbols you typed are entered into the active worksheet. Click any of the names for more details about the quote.

7 ▶ Save the workbook and close your Internet connection.

✓ **Import Other Data from the Web**

Other types of imported data are available on the Web. Click **Data, Get External Data, Run Web Query.** Then double-click **Get More Web Queries.iqy** in the Run Query dialog box. This places introductory information and a list of queries in your active worksheet. Scroll past the introductory information to see the list of Web queries.

⚠ **WARNING**

External data queries run flawlessly—most of the time. It's a good idea to save any other work before running a query, just in case.

✓ **Where to Get Multiple Stock Quotes**

If you don't have the Multiple Stock Quotes by PC Quote, Inc.iqy query in your Excel installation, check for it on your Office 97 CD. Or visit the PC Quote Web site at http://www.pcquote.com to download the query.

Create Worksheet Links

Hyperlinks are underlined words or phrases that take us from Web page to Web page on the World Wide Web. Similar links—to Web sites, documents on your hard drive, or even other sheets in the workbook—can be added to worksheets.

✓ **Edit Hyperlinks**
To edit a hyperlink, right-click the hyperlink text and choose **Hyperlink, Edit Hyperlink.**

✓ **Hyperlink to a Web Site or to Other Files**
To create a hyperlink to another file on your computer, company network, or the Web, click the **Browse** button next to the Link to File or URL text box in the Insert Hyperlink dialog box.

Task 3: Inserting Hyperlinks into Worksheets

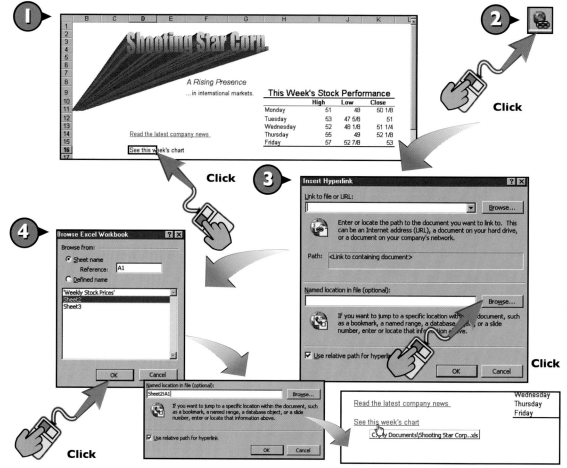

1 Select the cell containing the text you want to make into a hyperlink.

2 Click the **Insert Hyperlink** button on the Standard toolbar.

3 The Insert Hyperlink dialog box opens. To link to another sheet in the active workbook, click the **Browse** button next to the **Named Location in File** text box.

4 In the Browse Excel Workbook dialog box, click a sheet name and choose **OK**. When the Browse dialog box closes, choose **OK** again in the Insert Hyperlink dialog box.

Task 4: Saving Worksheets as Web Pages

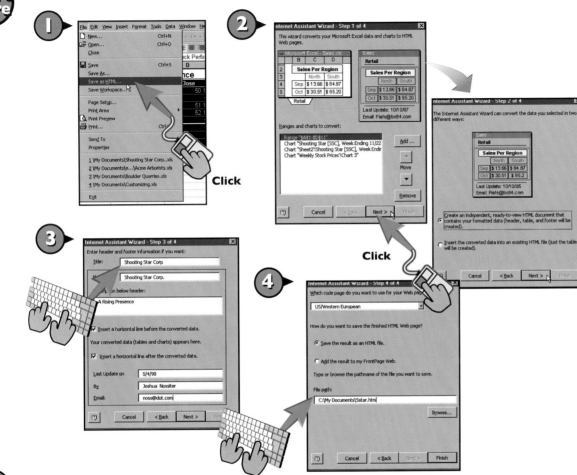

Click

Click

Worksheet Web Pages

HTML (Hypertext Markup Language) is the language of Web pages. Creating a Web page out of a worksheet means translating the worksheet into HTML, a job Excel does for you.

✓ **Viewing Web Pages Created from Excel Files**
To view a Web page that was created from an Excel file, choose **File, Open**. Locate the file and double-click the filename.

✓ **Formatting Lost?**
Many Excel features, including most formatting, gets lost in the conversion to HTML. Hyperlinks, however, are included in HTML documents produced by Excel.

⚠ **WARNING**
To select a cell containing a hyperlink, use the keyboard arrow keys. Using your mouse activates the hyperlink.

---

1. After you save your workbook as a regular Excel file, select the range you want to use as a Web page. Then choose **File, Save as HTML**.

2. The Internet Assistant Wizard appears. Choose Next to accept the default settings in the Step 1 of 4 and Step 2 of 4 dialog boxes.

3. In the Step 3 of 4 dialog box, the Internet Assistant uses the workbook name as a Web page title and the sheet name as a header. When you're ready, choose **Next**.

4. In the Step 4 of 4 dialog box, type a filename and pathname and click **Finish**.

Task 5: Importing Graphics from the Web

A World of Graphics on the WWW

If you find the clip art supplied with Excel inadequate, a quick trip to the World Wide Web gets you all the clip art you need.

✅ **Categorize Your Clip Art**
To move downloaded clip art into categories other than "Downloaded Clips," select the clip and choose **Clip Properties**. Click another category in the Clip Properties dialog box and choose **OK**.

✅ **Keep Checking the Gallery**
The clip art selections in the Microsoft Clip Gallery Live Web site change frequently, so return visits are worth the effort.

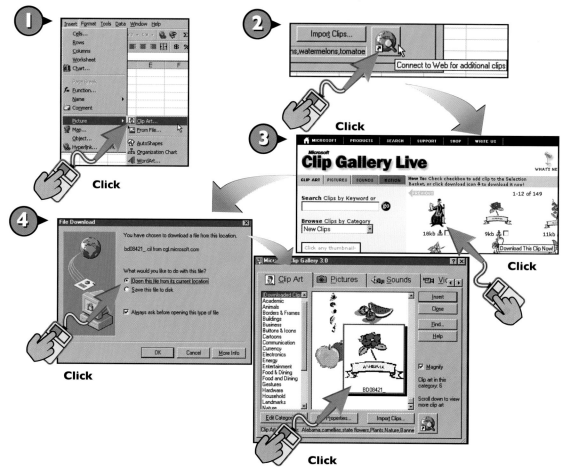

Click

Click

Connect to Web for additional clips

Click

Click

Click

Click

I Choose **Insert, Picture, Clip Art**.

2 In Microsoft Clip Gallery 3.0, click the **Connect to Web** button. Click **OK** if the Connect to Web message box appears.

3 Choose a clip from the New Clips category, or search by keyword or category to locate the clip you want. Click a clip to download the clip to your computer.

4 The File Download dialog box appears. Choose **Open This File from Its Current Location** and click **OK**.

Task 6: Getting Excel Help Online

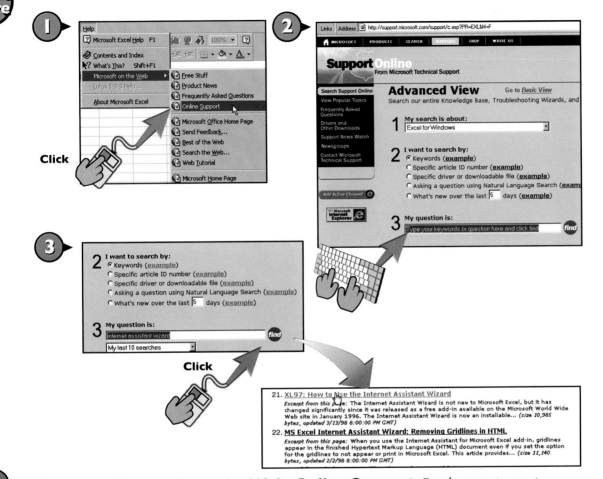

Help on the World Wide Web

When Excel's Help system (and this book) fails to answer your queries, get Excel Help from the Internet.

Start Here

Click

Click

✅ **Use Quotation Marks in Keyword Searches**
If you choose a keyword search—the default choice on the Online Support page—your search sometimes results in too many documents. If this happens, try typing a keyword phrase enclosed in quotation marks.

1. Click **Help, Microsoft on the Web, Online Support**. Excel connects you to the World Wide Web and loads the Microsoft Support Online page in your Web browser.

2. The Support Online page has three numbered areas in which you enter your search parameters. In area 1, type the subject of your search; in area 3, type your question.

3. Choose a "search by" option in area 2, and then click **Find**. Online Support displays a menu of articles that might be relevant to your search.

✅ **Microsoft FAQs**
If your Online Support searches yield nothing fruitful, try clicking **Help, Microsoft on the Web, Frequently Asked Questions.**

End Task

Absolute reference A cell reference that does not change, no matter where associated cells or formulas are moved on the worksheet. Indicated by dollar signs.

Active cell The currently selected cell, indicated by a thick border.

Arguments Values used by a function, generally cell references.

Axes Arms of a chart (see **Z axis**).

Category (X) axis The chart axis representing data categories, most commonly the horizontal axis of a chart.

Cell reference The cell address, defined by the column and row intersection where the cell is located.

Cells The intersection of a row and column, in which all Excel data is entered.

Chart objects All components of a chart, including axes, titles, and legend.

Chart sheets Charts placed on their own worksheets.

Column chart A chart displaying values vertically by category.

Column headings Lettered buttons at the top of worksheet columns. Click to select entire column.

Cone chart Like a column chart, but with cones instead of columns.

Cylinder chart Like a column chart, but with cylinders instead of columns.

Data points Individual values in a chart category, corresponding to worksheet cells.

Data series The range of chart values in a single category, corresponding to a worksheet row or column and indicated in the legend of a chart.

Doughnut chart A doughnut-shaped chart displaying the relationship between the parts and the whole. Related to pie charts but can display multiple series in concentric rings.

Field Individual item in a List record; can also refer to a text box in a dialog box.

Fill handle A small black box in the lower-right corner of a selected cell or range. Can be dragged to fill a series or copy cells.

Filters Criteria by which a list is displayed.

Fonts Type faces, such as Times New Roman or Courier.

Footer Text at the foot of a printed page that repeats on multiple pages.

Formula bar Area directly below the toolbars where data, formulas, and functions are entered and edited.

Formula palette Gray strip that appears when the Edit formula button is clicked, displaying the formula result. Can be dragged out of the way.

Functions Prefabricated formulas that come with Excel for performing most calculations. Accessed through the Formula bar or the Paste Function button.

Gridlines Vertical and horizontal lines that crisscross a worksheet or chart. Worksheet gridlines can be turned off from the Tools, Options menu.

Handle See **Selection handles**.

Header Text at the top of a printed page that repeats on multiple pages.

Header row Top row of a list, which labels the data in each column of the list.

HTML Hypertext Markup Language. A text and graphics formatting language standard on the World Wide Web.

Hyperlink Text or graphics (often underlined if text) containing an embedded Web or network address. When clicked, the hyperlink opens the document at the embedded address.

Landscape orientation   Page printed with the longer edges of the page at the top and bottom.

Legend   Key to a chart, indicating the data series.

Links   See **Hyperlink**.

Marquee   Moving border that appears around a cut or copied selection.

Name box   Located to the left of the Formula bar, the Name box displays the address of the selected cell or the name (in text) of the selected object. Can be used to name cells and ranges.

Nonadjacent cells or ranges Cells or ranges that are not side by side. Press the Ctrl key to select nonadjacent cells.

Page breaks   Points in the worksheet where Excel will end one printed page and begin another.

Pie chart   A chart displaying the relationship between the whole and the parts. Can display only one data series.

Portrait orientation   Page printed with the longer edges of the page at the left and right.

Pyramid   Like a column chart, but with pyramids instead of columns.

Range   Two or more cells, defined by the first and last cell in the range (for example, A3:G3).

Record   A complete list entry; a row composed of one or more fields.

Relative reference   A cell or range reference that changes as associated values or formulas are moved or copied across the worksheet.

Row headings   Numbered buttons at the beginning of every Excel row. Click to select the entire row.

Sans serif   Any style of type that lacks the short strokes at the beginning and end of characters, such as Arial.

Scatter chart   A chart displaying changing values at irregular intervals over time.

Scientific notation   A format displayed by Excel when the column is not wide enough to display an entire number.

ScreenTip   An identifying label displayed onscreen when the pointer is aimed at toolbar buttons, chart objects, and such.

Scroll box   Square or rectangular control that slides along scrollbars. Drag to scroll the worksheet variable amounts.

Scroll buttons   Arrow buttons at either end of a scrollbar. Click to scroll the worksheet one row or column at a time.

Scrollbars   Vertical and horizontal strips at the right and bottom of the worksheet that, when clicked, move the worksheet up, down, or sideways so you can see additional data.

Selection handles   Square or rectangular markers that appear around a selected object. Can be dragged to move or resize objects.

Series   See **Data series**.

Sheet tab   A tab-shaped button at the bottom of a worksheet. Click to change the active worksheet. Double-click to rename the worksheet.

Shortcut menu   Menu that appears when the right mouse button is clicked.

Splash screen   A program's opening screen, which displays while the program loads.

Split bar   A small bar-shaped control at the top of the vertical scroll bar and the right end of the horizontal scrollbar. Drag to divide the screen into independently scrollable panes.

Status bar Located at the bottom of the Excel window directly below the sheet tabs; displays information about the worksheet.

Tick marks Lines marking values and categories along the axes of a chart.

Title bar Colored title of windows and dialog boxes; can be dragged to move the window or box.

URL Universal Resource Locator. World Wide Web address, often in the form http://www.domain.com.

Value (Y) axis The chart axis displaying data values on which the chart is based, most commonly the vertical axis.

Web browser Software used to display and navigate among documents on the World Wide Web.

X axis See **Category (X) axis**.

Y axis See **Value (Y) axis**.

Z axis The equivalent of the Y axis in a 3D chart.

Index

Symbols

Index